The Arno Press Cinema Program

THE
LEGION OF DECENCY
A Sociological Analysis
of the
Emergence and Development
of a
Social Pressure Group

Paul W. Facey

ARNO PRESS
A NEW YORK TIMES COMPANY
New York • 1974

This volume was selected for the
Dissertations on Film Series
of the ARNO PRESS CINEMA PROGRAM
by Garth S. Jowett, Carleton University

First publication in book form, Arno Press, 1974

Copyright © 1974 by Paul W. Facey

THE ARNO PRESS CINEMA PROGRAM
For complete listing of cinema titles see last pages

Manufactured in the United States of America

— — — — — — — — — — — — — —

Library of Congress Cataloging in Publication Data

Facey, Paul W   1909-
    The Legion of Decency.

    (Dissertations on film series of the Arno Press
cinema program)
    Originally presented as the author's thesis.
    1. National Legion of Decency. 2. Moving-
pictures--Moral and religious aspects. 3. Moving-
pictures--Censorship--United States. I. Title.
II. Series: Dissertations on film series.
PN1995.5.F27 1974   301.5'7   73-21596
ISBN 0-405-04871-8

THE LEGION OF DECENCY: A SOCIOLOGICAL

ANALYSIS OF THE EMERGENCE AND

DEVELOPMENT OF A SOCIAL PRESSURE GROUP

BY

PAUL W. FACEY, S.J.
B.A., Boston College, '31
M.A., Boston College, '32

DISSERTATION
SUBMITTED IN PARTIAL FULFILLMENT OF THE REQUIREMENTS FOR
THE DEGREE OF DOCTOR OF PHILOSOPHY IN THE DEPARTMENT OF
POLITICAL PHILOSOPHY AT FORDHAM UNIVERSITY

NEW YORK
1945

TABLE OF CONTENTS

LIST OF TABLES

THE LEGION OF DECENCY:

A SOCIOLOGICAL ANALYSIS OF THE EMERGENCE

AND DEVELOPMENT OF A SOCIAL PRESSURE GROUP

CHAPTER I

INTRODUCTION

The Social Problem of the Motion Picture

Motion picture entertainment is only fifty years old. Yet during its short lifetime it has posed a social problem which has been a concern of millions of Americans. Society has solved this problem in a way which is of considerable sociological interest. After many years of trial-and-error attempts at a solution, there has been worked out a unique process which combines industry self-control with the supporting pressure of a group organized under the leadership of a religious body, the whole process completely by-passing the police power of the state.

This study will analyze the process of the emergence and the structure of one part of this combination: namely, the pressure group which is called the Legion of Decency.[1]

Preliminary consideration must be given to the nature of the motion picture problem, and of the attempts to solve it which preceded the advent of the Legion of Decency. Also, certain sociological concepts which will form the frame of reference for the analysis must be explained and clarified. These are the two subjects of this introductory chapter.

─────────────────────────────────────

1. Ruth A. Inglis, "The Hays office control of motion picture content" (Unpublished Ph.D. dissertation, Bryn Mawr, 1945), provides an exhaustive study of the other part of the process: the industry's self-control system.

The magnitude of the problem

Some indication of the extent to which the motion pictures have become a part of the contemporary culture may be gathered from the fact that a leading figure of the film industry could make, in all seriousness, this statement: "The motion picture is the epitome of civilization and the quintessence of what we mean by 'America'".[1] Superlatives are known to be a debased coinage in movieland. Yet even the leader of a world-wide religious body, writing in very sober style, testifies that "the motion picture has become the most popular form of diversion which is offered for the leisure moments, not only of the rich, but of all classes of society."[2] Any social problem connected with the motion pictures directly affects millions of people, because of the peculiar conjunction of the facts that the films reach an enormous audience, and that this vast audience subsists upon almost identical film fare.

Size of the film public.--Commercial moving picture entertainment began, in 1894, with the "peep-show."[3] One customer at a time paid for the privilege of looking through the lens of a Thomas A. Edison Kinetoscope at some fifty feet of "moving" pictures photographed on continuous film. Two years later the pictures were projected from the

---

1. Will H. Hays, See and hear, Motion Picture Producers and Distributors of America, Inc., 1929, p. 4.
2. Pope Pius XI, Encyclical letter on motion pictures (trans.), Washington, D.C., National Catholic Welfare Conference, 1936, p. 8.
3. For the early history of the motion pictures this chapter relies chiefly on Terry Ramsaye, A million and one nights, 2 vols., New York, Simon and Schuster, 1926.

film onto a screen, and many people could see the same picture at the same time. At first they were shown only in vaudeville houses; they obtained homes of their own when "nickelodeons", charging five cents for a fifteen minute program, began to spring up in vacant stores and in the penny arcades of large cities. A nickelodeon accomodated from twenty-five to a few hundred patrons. This was in 1905 and the succeeding years. In 1914, Samuel L. Rothafel, the famous "Roxy", directed the opening of the Strand Theatre, on Broadway in New York. It was the pioneer exclusively motion picture theater. The movies were on their way to cater to the huge audiences of the future. Eight years after the Strand opened, there were 15,000 theaters showing motion pictures in the United States, with a seating capacity of over 7,500,000.[1] In 1942, there were 112 movie palaces which could seat 3,000 or more people at a time.[2] In that same year movies were shown to an estimated 85,000,000 people each week.[3] Fifty percent of the nation's children, and almost forty percent of its adults go to the movies once every week.[4]

In less than fifty years the movies achieved the distinction of being the most widely popular form of entertainment in the world's history.

Identity of film fare.--A handful of producing companies make almost all the pictures patronized by this tremendous audience; and the pictures are substantially the same for all.

---

1. Film facts 1942, New York, Motion Picture Producers and Distributors of America, Inc., 1942, p. 11.
2. Ibid., p. 8.
3. Ibid., p. 9.
4. Fortune, XIII (1936), 222.

The story of the concentration of the motion picture business in
the hands of a few companies has been told at length, and brilliantly,
by Terry Ramsaye.[1] The industry started its career primarily as a
machinery business, bent on making its profits by renting patented
projection machines and licensed film to go with them. Early attempts
to monopolize this business were successfully fought by independents,
who thereupon proceeded to wage a relentless competitive war upon each
other. Producers offered fabulous salaries to stars and directors, in
attempts to corner the production market. Exhibitors became producers.
Producers bought up distributing agencies. Producer-distributors bought
or built more and more theaters. After bewildering years of mergers,
bankruptcies and the fiercest sort of competition, eight companies
have survived as the major producing companies in the United States.[2]
All of these eight are also in the distributing business, and five of
them own their own chains of theaters, as well.[3] Apart from the
question of the control they may exercise over the smaller companies,
the member companies of this small group determine the type of film
entertainment which the American public may enjoy.[4]

If it were possible, these producers would like every member of
the large movie audience to see every picture they produce. With the
exception of the cowboy, Western pictures, each picture produced aims
to please everybody. This is not merely a case of the profit motive in

1. Ramsaye, op. cit., passim.
2. Paramount Pictures, Inc., Loew's, Inc. (Metro-Goldwyn-Mayer),
   Twentieth Century-Fox Film Corporation, Warner Brothers Pictures,
   Inc., Radio-Keith-Orpheum Corporation, Universal Corporation,
   Columbia Pictures Corporation and United Artists Corporation.
3. U. S. Congress, Temporary national economic committee, The motion
   picture industry--a pattern of control, Monograph No. 43, Washington,
   D.C., Government Printing Office, 1941, pp. 59 ff.
4. Cf. ibid., pp. 8 ff.

the colossal proportions typical of Hollywood; it is an economic necessity. A motion picture costs so much that it must reach a wide audience to make any profit. The enormous salaries paid to stars and directors and executives, plus the high costs of the technical side of production, result in extremely large budgets for production costs, running into hundreds of thousands of dollars, even at times into millions of dollars for a single picture.[1] As the average admission fee is only about twenty-five cents,[2] hundreds of thousands of people must see the picture if it is to make any money. As a result the movies have become a truly mass medium of communication, quite unlike the theater or the press, which offer diverse cultural products to differentiated audiences.

The moral problem

Movies as entertainment.--The communication for which the motion pictures are the medium has been almost exclusively limited to the field of entertainment. Newsreels and "educational" subjects form a small proportion of the total output; problems which have arisen in connection with them will not be included in this study. The Legion of Decency restricts its activity to "feature" entertainment pictures to the almost absolute exclusion of all others.

The first movies provided entertainment of a sort simply by virtue of the fact that people enjoyed the novelty of seeing other people and objects pictured in motion. What it was that moved was of secondary

---

1. Compare with the initial production cost of $18,000 for the hit production on Broadway, "Yes, My Darling Daughter." Fortune, XVII (1938), 106.
2. Film Facts 1942, p. 7.

importance; motion was the primary attraction, and it still is a fundamental source of appeal. The first subjects of the quarter-minute
peep-shows were bits of vaudeville acts: tumblers, contortionists,
dancers and the like. The films later projected onto the screens of
vaudeville stages depicted, for the space of twelve or fourteen minutes,
similar novelties, plus items of current interest, such as parades, and
pictures of the scenic wonders like Niagara Falls. Thought content
was nil. The first successful attempt to tell a story in the movies
was the famous picture The Great Train Robbery, in 1903. In the
scramble for successors to this melodramatic thriller, the files of
contemporary dime novels were racked. Nickelodeons were filled with
patrons of these pictures. Then foreign films of the Quo Vadis type
were imported and played in legitimate theaters. These were mostly
spectacle and pageantry. A turning point as regards film content came
with The Birth of a Nation which combined spectacle and action with
the skillful narration of a full length story. In addition, there
were controversies regarding the film's portrayal of the negro question
which brought the moving picture to the attention of large numbers of
people who had had no contact with the nickelodeon pictures. For the
next fifteen years the movies told in pantomime all manners of stories,
always with the emphasis upon visual elements rather than on thought
content. But when sound was successfully synchronized with action
toward the end of the 1920's, the movies broadened the scope of their
entertainment possibilities. The drama of dialogue, its wit, humor,
and above all its superior capacity for communicating ideas added
tremendously to the thought-provoking character of film entertainment.

The coming of sound helped to still the objections of those who considered the movies to be inferior intellectual pabulum, too trashy for serious consideration. But it also provided new opportunities to arouse the displeasure of those who objected to film content from a moral point of view.

Objection to movie morality.--From the very beginning of their brief career, the movies have incurred the hostility of people concerned with their moral implications and their effect upon the patrons. In 1895, a Kinetoscope film entitled "Dolorita's Passion Dance" and a fifty-foot picture called "The May Irwin - John C. Rice Kiss" provoked squalls of disapproval. In 1907, the city of Chicago enacted the first municipal censorship ordinance directed against the nickelodeon thrillers. Seven years later, in defence of the censors, The Northwestern Christian Advocate cited as "one day's batch of excised scenes":

> The Hopi Raiders--Killing soldier in fort and picket at gate. Shorten scene of dead bodies. The Chest of Fortune-- Hitting man on head, taking records, and putting body in dredge-scoop. Pirate of the Plains--Posse shooting against sheriff and display of dead bodies. Shorten shooting scenes to a flash. Paradise Lost--From point at which second man enters house to where he leaves woman in bedroom. A Romance of the Northwest--Two gambling scenes. Shorten time man's head is held under water. Mario--Stabbing man at wedding and struggle between man and girl. His Faithful Passion--Kidnapping girl. Shorten showing of man with skull crushed and death-bed scene. The Warning--Hold-up, taking gun, locking girl in closet, cutting rope, and tying man. The Heart of Carito--Flogging of girl.[1]

Objection to the crude brutalities of the one-reel thrillers was succeeded by objection to sex behavior portrayed in the feature length pictures. There were the "vampire" pictures, just before the turn of

---

1. Quoted in Literary Digest, XLVIII (March 28, 1914), 702.

the 1920's; the most renowned "vamp" was Theda Bara, "foreign, volup-
tuous and fatal."[1] There were the "sheik" pictures of the early 1920's,
featuring players like Rudolph Valentino, and "full of sex and romantic
adventures in distant places."[2] The latter half of the decade saw
Clara Bow, the "It Girl", "an almost sexless figure around whom conversations about sex continually raged."[3] Then a number of actresses of
the Marlene Dietrich type, "playing the ideal mistress, silken, lustrous,
unbelievably handsome."[4] And, just before the Legion of Decency, there
were the unique portrayals by Mae West, "vigorous, downright,
artistically fraudulent"[5] burlesques of the laughable prostitute with
the famous catch-line "come up and see me some time."

Except for the Mae West pictures, it was generally true that as
the movies matured, in content and in technique, the cruder
violations of the standards of sex behavior gave way to the more
subtle. The coming of talking pictures accentuated the trend, opening
the door, through dialogue, to a wider horizon of ideas than could be
conveyed by the pantomime of the silent films. The attractions of
the "vamps", the "sheiks", the "it girls", had been predominantly in
the visual, the sense realm. True, the themes, the "lessons" of these
pictures had been attacked on moral grounds. But talking pictures,
keeping the visual elements of the earlier pictures, had added a greater
degree of sophistication, and there appeared a greater emphasis upon

---

1. Gilbert Seldes, The movies come from America, New York, Charles
   Scribner's Sons, 1937, p. 32.
2. Ibid., p. 30.
3. Ibid., p. 33.
4. Ibid.
5. Ibid., p. 34.

objection to the immorality of the ideas which it was claimed the movies were inculcating into their patrons. The charge that "evil is made to appear good" became the feature objection.

The cycle of gangster pictures of the early 30's became a storm center of objection on the grounds that they taught methods of crime in explicit detail, and glamorized the lives of criminals. They were the sophisticated counterparts of the one-reelers which had long ago aroused the ire of Chicago.

As the Legion of Decency drive was opening in 1934, Father Daniel A. Lord, S.J. published his analysis of 133 feature pictures released between January and May of that year by the leading producers. Father Lord objected to the following:

> 26 plots or episodes built on illicit love, i.e., love outside of marriage.
> 13 plots or main episodes were based on seduction accomplished.
> 12 plots or episodes presented seduction as attempted or planned.
> 2 had episodes based on rape.
> 1 went to the extreme of building on attempted incest.
> 18 characters, mostly all leading characters, lived in open adultery.
> 7 characters were shown planning or attempting adultery.
> 3 presented prostitutes as leading characters. (Prostitutes as incidental characters were frequent.)[1]

Such, in general, were the typical objections to the moral values of the movies. This subject will be given more detailed treatment in the course of the study.

---

1. Daniel A. Lord, S.J., The motion pictures betray America, St. Louis, The Queen's Work, Inc., 1934, p. 8 f.

Previous Attempts at Control

Informal Control

There is, for all cultural products, an informal social control
over their production, based upon the free acceptance or rejection of
the products by "the public", i.e., by the unorganized totality of the
potential users of the products.[1] There has always been such control
over motion picture production. The well known existence of movie
"cycles", which try to reduplicate types of pictures that have been
popular, is an instance. The disappearance of the slapstick comedy
in deference to the public's rejection of this type of picture is
another instance.

Yet the evidence shows that at various times in the history of
the motion picture in America, while there have been large-scale
objections to the films, people continued to go to the movies. That
the objections were not always confined to the non-movie-going public
appears from the fact that in the Legion of Decency times, people who
pledged themselves to stay away from objectionable pictures demanded
to know in advance which pictures were to be so classified. The
reason for this situation seems to be rooted in the fact that people
"go to the movies" without knowing in advance what sort of picture
they are going to see, and they keep "going to the movies" despite
repeated experiences of sitting through dull or offensive films.
Fortune's survey showed that 46.7 percent of the people in this country
go to see "any good" film without much forethought.[2] As Seldes says,

---

1. Cf. N. S. Timasheff, "The Legal regimentation of culture in National
   Socialist Germany," Fordham law review, XI (1942), 1.
2. Fortune, XIII (1936), 222.

"The fundamental passion is a desire to go to the movies, which means
to go to any movie rather than not go at all."[1] Moreover, outside the
larger communities the millions who go at least once a week have little
or no opportunity to discriminate; in the smaller communities there is
only one picture house available. They see whatever happens to be
showing. No doubt some pictures attract larger audiences than others.
No doubt the local exhibitor tries to cater to what he believes to be
the tastes of his community. But the motion picture industry, after
fifty years of effort, is still looking for the system which will tell
them just why one picture succeeds where another fails at the box-
office. So far is the industry from a complete understanding of what
the people want. The informal control by audiences has not spared
them the torment of dull pictures. Sporadic outbursts of moral
indignation showed that up to the time of the Legion of Decency informal
control had not succeeded in eliminating offensive pictures.

Formal Control

Until the organization of the Hays office began to exercise control,
formal control had been attempted through public and private censorship.

Public censorship.--The police power of several politically
organized communities has been engaged to suppress the showing of
pictures considered to be morally objectionable.[2]

Municipalities, following the example of the Chicago ordinance of
1907, have in many instances specifically entrusted the control of

1. Seldes, op. cit., p. 13.
2. Ford H. MacGregor, "Official censorship legislation," The annals,
   CXXVIII (November, 1926), 170-173.

movies to the police or to specially designated individuals or commissions. This is an addition to the general police power and welfare clauses which enable a municipality to suppress any indecent or improper entertainment. In the majority of these cases, there is no provision for previous censorship.

A half dozen states,[1] beginning with Pennsylvania in 1911, have enacted film censorship legislation which prevents the showing within the state of films not previously approved by the official censors. Ohio and Kansas enacted such legislation in 1913; Maryland in 1916; New York in 1921; Virginia in 1922. Florida enacted a law in 1921 making the showing of pictures contingent upon the approval of the National Board of Review. The law is not enforced. Massachusetts defeated by referendum censorship legislation in 1922; but in that state pictures to be shown on Sundays must be approved by an official censor.

The federal government exercises no censorship over the moral content of the Hollywood product.[2] The Treasury Department is empowered to forbid the importation into this country of films which are morally offensive, or obscene. It has not chosen to exercise this power frequently. Federal legislation has also forbidden interstate traffic to films depicting prize-fights, has forbidden film-makers to derogate the uniform of the United States military forces, and the government has, in recent years, used pressure to prevent the production of films

---

1. MacGregor, "Official censorship legislation," The annals,CXXVIII (November, 1926), 166-170.
2. Ibid., 163-166. Cf. Comment, "Censorship of motion pictures," The Yale law journal, XLIX (1939), 87-113; also Kadin, "Administrative censorship," Boston University law review, XIX (1939), 561 ff.

which might inculcate pacifism.[1] But all attempts to give the federal
government control over the morals of the movies through federal
censorship legislation have failed to pass in Congress.

Private Control

Alongside the public, political agencies just described, there
has existed for years a private organization attempting to exercise
influence over the content of the films. It has made use of two
methods of control. In its early years, when it was called the
National Board of Censorship of Motion Pictures, this private group,
which had been organized at the request of the nascent industry in
1909 as a defense against encroaching legislation,[2] actually had the
power to control the moral content of the motion pictures. The
industry had agreed to abide by its decisions, and it rejected many
offensive pictures in toto, and deleted objectionable items from
countless others. After a half dozen years of this work, the National
Board abandoned its policy of previous censorship, for reasons which
have never been made clear.[3] Under a new name, the National Board of
Review of Motion Pictures, it adopted the policy of giving its approval
to almost all pictures, reserving superior approbation to pictures of
"special merit." Thus it was said that larger audiences would be
attracted to the "better" pictures, and the other sort would die of
malpatronage.

Until the Hays office was organized in 1922, then, formal control

1. Variety, August 2, 1939; Box office, September 22, 1939.
2. Report of the National Board of Censorship of Motion Pictures, New
York, 1911 and succeeding years through 1916.
3. The National Board of Review of Motion Pictures--how it works, New
York, n.d., p. 8.

of the morals of the movies was limited to the scattered efforts of a
few municipal and state agencies, along with the "praise the best, ignore
the rest" activities of the National Board of Review. That the
industry found it necessary to organize and bring in Will H. Hays as
its head is sufficient indication that this control was not satisfactory
to a formidable number of people.

Self Control

A motion picture trade association had been formed in 1916, under
the name of the National Association of the Motion Picture Industry.
It suffered from inept leadership and the lack of whole-hearted moral
and financial support of the fiercely competitive members of the
industry.[1] It proved itself unable to turn back the rising tide of
political censorship legislation.

At the beginning of the 1920's a series of scandals in the private
lives of some of Hollywood's most noted figures brought to the boiling
point the long-simmering indignation of those who thought the movies a
menace to morals. Mary Pickford, "America's Sweetheart", divorced Owen
Moore and quickly married Douglas Fairbanks; all were stars of the
first rank, Pickford being at the very top. Fatty Arbuckle, the
screen's funny man, became involved in an unpleasant charge of
manslaughter in connection with what was described as an orgiastic party.
Wallace Reid, a favorite leading man died under suspicious circumstances
pointed to the use of drugs. And there were other scandals which placed
Hollywood in the public eye as the modern rival of Sodom and Gommorah.

1. Inglis, op. cit., pp. 67-73.

Protest became organized through the channels of women's clubs, civic and religious groups.[1] The Literary Digest, May 14, 1921, commented:

> There is no longer any dispute as to whether purification is needed...all the magazine and newspaper discussion as to whether there is a "movie menace" shifts to a hot debate in the press and among our legislators over how the reform is to come.[2]

The same article announced the industry's defense: the promise of the powerless National Association of the Motion Picture Industry that the industry would abide by a new code of moral standards. But New York State went ahead with its censorship law, and Congress had before it a resolution to investigate the entire motion picture industry. The movie magnates decided upon drastic measures. Swallowing the extremes of their competitive differences, they agreed upon the organization of a real trade association to replace the nominal NAMPI. In imitation of the professional baseball industry which had hired the famed Judge Landis to lend an aura of respectability to the sport after a damaging bribery scandal, Will H. Hays was invited to head the reorganized trade association. Hays was then the Postmaster General in the Harding Cabinet; he had been chairman of the Republican National Committee in the successful election of the year before; he was a respected lay leader in the affairs of the Presbyterian Church. The new organization, whose official title is the Motion Picture Producers and Distributors of America, Inc., has always been known simply as "The Hays Office."

The invitation tendered to Hays makes it clear that the industry's principal anxiety was to improve the public relations so damaged by the

---

1. Fortune, XVIII (1938), 72.
2. Literary Digest, LXIX (May 14, 1921), 32.

current wave of scandals.

> The undersigned...realize the necessity for attaining
> and maintaining the highest possible standards of motion
> picture film production in this country and are striving
> to have the industry accorded the consideration and
> dignity to which it is justly entitled, and proper repre-
> sentation before the people of this country so that its
> position, at all times, may be presented in an unbiased
> and unprejudiced manner.
> We realize that in order that we will have proper
> contact with the general public and to retain its confi-
> dence, and in order to attain complete accord in our
> industry, that it will be necessary to obtain the services
> of one who has already, by his outstanding achievements,
> won the confidence of the people of this country, and who,
> by his ability as an organizer and executive, has won the
> confidence, admiration, and respect of the people in the
> motion picture industry....[1]

Nothing in the letter suggests that Hays was to have dictatorial
power over motion picture content similar to the power exercised by
Landis in the baseball world. Yet Hays was popularly known as the
"czar" of the film industry, and it was to the industry's interest to
have the public think that he was holding a strong rein on the
producers. It was not until the Legion of Decency campaign that the
industry admitted that Hays had not reigned supreme. R. H. Cochrane,
vice-president of Universal Pictures Corporation then wrote, "So the
Church drive has served a good purpose. It has placed in the hands
of Mr. Hays the power that he was popularly supposed to have, but
never did have."[2]

Although Hays had neither the authority nor the machinery to

---

1. Letter to W. H. Hays, signed by leaders of the industry, December 2, 1941. Reproduced in Ramsaye, op. cit., vol. 2, p. 813; emphasis inserted.
2. New York World-telegram, August 13, 1934. Cf. Eric M. Knight, "The movie 'czar'," Philadelphia evening public ledger, August 25, 1934.

effect sweeping changes in the moral content of the pictures, his organization did take some steps which paved the way toward ultimate self-regulation supported by organized pressure from society. The final stages in the creation of the self-regulation process begin with the acceptance of the Production Code by the industry in 1930; they are treated in this study as the initial stages in the emergence of the Legion of Decency. The preliminary steps may be indicated here.

Hays assumed office in March, 1922. In September of that year, a representative of the Hays office was authorized to review pictures before they were released.[1] The reviewers were not, however, authorized to dictate any changes in the films. As the Hollywood staff of the Hays office then consisted of not more than a handful of people,[2] and Hays' major activity was improvement of public relations and opposition to censorship legislation, this was a very thin entering wedge.

The first actual step toward self-regulation came two years later, with the introduction of "The Formula," the resolution which set up machinery to regulate the production of pictures based on stories and plays liable to be the occasion of moral objection. This was "the initial move of the industry, after the formation of the Hays organization, in the direction of self-discipline with respect to the moral quality of its product."[3]

---

1. Inglis, op. cit., p. 86.
2. Fortune, XVIII (December, 1938), 140.
3. The public relations of the motion picture industry, a report by the department of research and education, Federal Council of the Churches of Christ in America, New York, 1931, p. 124. Cf. Hays, See and hear, p. 28.

Next came the promulgation of the "Don'ts" and "Be Carefuls" in 1927. The Hays office had studied the eliminations made by the various official censorship boards. Finding a certain common denominator in them, it listed eleven items which "shall not appear in pictures produced by members" of the Hays group, "irrespective of the manner in which they are treated." Twenty-six other subjects were listed to be treated with "special care," "to the end that vulgarity and suggestiveness may be eliminated and that good taste may be emphasized."[1] In October, 1927, this list of "Don'ts" and "Be Carefuls" was officially adopted in a resolution of the Motion Picture Producers and Distributors of America, Inc.

Noteworthy, however, was the fact that no machinery for enforcement of the resolution was set up. In 1929 the studio relations department of the Hays office, then headed by Jason S. Joy, was consulted by seven of the nine member producing companies respecting ninety-four of the four hundred and eighty-nine pictures produced by them. Of three hundred and eighty-four detailed suggestions, two hundred and fifteen were accepted, one hundred and sixty-nine were rejected.[2]

Such was the self-control situation on the eve of the introduction of the Production Code.

The position of pressure groups concerned with movie morality changed considerably during the interval between 1922 and 1929. The first change came with the establishment in June, 1922, of the Public

1. Rule 21 of the code of the motion picture industry, adopted at the Trade Practice Conference for the Motion Picture Industry, held under the auspices of the Federal Trade Commission, New York City, October 10 to 15, 1927, New York, n.d.
2. The public relations of the motion picture industry, p. 126.

Relations Committee.[1] Among the sixty or more organizations represented on the Committee were: National Society of the Sons of the American Revolution, National Educational Association, Federal Council of the Churches of Christ in America, the International Committee of the Y.M.C.A., Boy Scouts of America, Girl Scouts of America, The American Legion, American Federation of Labor, the National Community Center Association, Camp Fire Girls, the American Sunday School Union, Chatauqua Institute, Daughters of the American Revolution, National Board of the Y.W.C.A., International Federation of Catholic Alumnae, Russell Sage Foundation, Central Conference of American Rabbis, Associated Advertising Clubs of the World, National Catholic Welfare Conference, and the American Library Association. The Committee's purpose was to "improve" film content. Its method was to channel complaints through the Committee to the Hays office, and at the same time to promote the wider patronage of approved pictures.

The professional reform organizations were not on the committee. There is little doubt that Hays' idea was to guide criticism in the direction where it could do the least harm. As Ramsaye says, "One of the important functions of the Hays office is to listen to people with a pain about the screen. It gives an outlet to shouting that used to be done in the newspapers."[2] The resignation of many of the affiliates of this Committee in the succeeding years indicates that there was not unanimous satisfaction with the results of the complaints. But the formation of the Committee was a significant step insofar as it bestowed status upon group complaints; it was an acknowledgement by the

1. Hays, op. cit., p. 29; Inglis, op. cit., pp. 86 ff.
2. Ramsaye, op. cit., vol. 2, p. 820.

industry of its recognition of the right of groups to bring social pressure to bear upon its activities.

The Public Relations Committee was dissolved in 1925, and was replaced by the Department of Public Relations, which was an integral part of the Hays office.[1] It still functions as such. The significant step taken by the Department was the extension to private groups, formerly connected with the old Public Relations Committee, of facilities to preview pictures before they were released to the public. Some of the previewing groups--the International Federation of Catholic Alumnae among them--issued critiques of the films. The Hays office cooperated financially in the distribution of these critiques. They were confined to pictures which merited approval; other pictures were not mentioned. This step is significant because it provided machinery whereby social pressure groups could mobilize their followers in advance of the release of any picture. Hitherto pressure had always come after the offending picture had been shown to the public. This machinery was later used by the Legion of Decency.

The Control Situation in 1929

This was the situation, then, in 1929.

1. Motion pictures offered a universal, mass audience form of entertainment.

2. The bulk of the pictures were produced by a small, organized group of producers.

---

1. Hays, op. cit., p. 30.

3. The moral content of the films was subject to varying degrees of control from (a) informal audience control; (b) formal control of a few public, official censors on the municipal and state levels; (c) organized pressure on a "praise the best, ignore the rest" basis from the National Board of Review and the groups affiliated with the Hays office Department of Public Relations; and (d) such self-control as was exercised through the Hays office Studio Relations Department on the basis of a code derived empirically from observation of censorship activities.

4. Objection to the moral qualities of the motion pictures continued to be voiced.

Into this situation a new factor entered toward the end of 1929. The development of that factor into the present system of industry self-control buttressed by organized social pressure will be the subject of the study which is to follow.

Relevant Sociological Concepts

A scientific sociological analysis must be made within the framework of concepts which are defined as rigidly as possible. To that end there must be introduced here the necessary clarification of what is understood in this study to be the meaning of the concepts "social control", "pressure groups" and the "structure of social action."

Social Control

The concept of social control has been worked over by many sociologists in recent years. Almost twenty-five years elapsed between Ross's Social Control,[1] the first book in the field, and Lumley's Means

---

1. Edward A. Ross, Social control, New York, The Macmillan Co., 1901.

of Social Control.[1] But in the past decade, Ross' work has been reissued, and there have been new studies by Bonney,[2] Dowd,[3] Landis,[4] Bernard,[5] and Pound.[6] Practically all textbooks on General Sociology treat the subject explicitly.

Despite this increase in attention, or perhaps because of it, agreement has grown less as to the precise definition of the concept. The interest shown in the field indicates that there is an underlying reality which deserves investigation. But so far efforts to isolate that reality so as to bring forth a useful concept, an efficient tool for future analysis, have failed.

A wider field of reality is embraced by a concept which comprehends fewer individuating qualities. Each qualification added to a concept restricts the range of its application. Thus, the concept "organized society" has greater comprehension, but less extension, than that of "society." The old rule of formal logic is "The greater the comprehension, the less the extension."

Herein lies the fundamental problem regarding the concept of social control. The principal disagreement concerns the propriety, or usefulness, of including in the concept the notion of purpose and the notion of social order. Some sociologists make use of a concept of social control which includes neither purposeful activity nor resultant social order.

1. Frederick E. Lumley, Means of social control, New York, The Century Company, 1925.
2. Merle E. Bonney, Techniques of appeal and of social control, Ph.D. dissertation, New York, Columbia University, 1934.
3. Jerome Dowd, Control in human societies, New York, D. Appleton-Century Company, Inc., 1936.
4. Paul H. Landis, Social control, New York, The Macmillan Co., 1939.
5. L. L. Bernard, Social control, New York, The Macmillan Co., 1939.
6. Roscoe Pound, Social control through law, New Haven, Yale University Press, 1942.

Others include purpose, but do not include social order. Vice versa, some include social order, but do not include purpose. And there are those who make the concept comprehend both purpose and social order. In order to formulate the concept to be used in this study, two questions must be answered. First, does the concept include the notion of purpose? Second, does the concept include the notion of social order?

Social control as purposeful activity.--There are two sets of authors who refuse to narrow the extension of the concept of social control by including in it the note of purposeful activity.

Eubank and Bernard make its extension so broad as to include "all the ways human beings influence each other."[1] Thus Bernard, having defined control as "a process by which stimuli are brought to bear effectively upon some person or group of persons, thus producing responses that function in adjustment,"[2] extends the concept of social control to "all types of control processes...operating between individuals and between individuals and groups,..."[3]

Others who, unlike Eubank and Bernard, limit the extension of the concept to activity which is productive of social order, agree with them that the concept is not limited to purposeful activity. These authors stress the function of impersonal factors such as usages, standards, values, culturally defined goals, etc., in molding the personality of the socialized, i.e., controlled individual. Thus, for

1. Earle E. Eubank, The concepts of sociology, New York, D. C. Heath and Company, 1932, p. 218.
2. Bernard, op. cit., p. 11.
3. Ibid., p. 12.

Landis, social control is "the personality-forming process through which original nature is passed";[1] it is "the socialization of the individual,"[2] which is accomplished principally through the "non-rational, unconscious, all-pervasive influences that mold the individual without his knowledge."[3] Hankins, too, stresses the impersonal process of attitude formation through conditioned responses;[4] "the average individual lives most of the time wholly unaware of social control"[5] exercised in this way. The concept of social control, he says, extends to "all those processes and instrumentalities by which the behavior of individuals is brought into conformity with social ideals and purposes."[6] So Reuter, although he is not altogether clear on the point, leans in the same direction when he says, "true social control is self-control";[7] this must mean that the concept of active social control extends to all the social factors, purposeful or not, which induce sentiments or standards into the socialized personality.

Bain offers vigorous objection to the non-purposeful concept.

> Social control should refer to definite rational attempts to get people and/or groups to behave in certain ways; it should not refer to all phases of the adaptation, adjustment, socialization, and interaction of human beings. Landis (and others) make it an omnium gatherum....[8]

Bain, in his insistence that the note of purpose be included in the

---

1. Landis, op. cit., p. 48.
2. Ibid., pp. 337 f.
3. Ibid., p. 13.
4. Frank H. Hankins, An introduction to the study of society, (rev. ed.), New York, The Macmillan Company, 1934, p. 388.
5. Ibid.
6. Ibid., p. 387.
7. Edward B. Reuter, Handbook of sociology, New York, The Dryden Press, 1941, p. 103.
8. Read Bain, rev. of Landis, Social control, American sociological review, IV (1939), 733.

comprehension of the concept, is repeating Lumley's definition:
"social control means getting others to do, believe, think, feel,...as
we wish them to,... In short, it is effective will-transference."[1]
Lumley, in this respect, agreed with Ross who had limited his extension
of the concept of social control to that domination of the individual
by society "which is intended and which fulfills a function in the life
of society."[2] Others who, explicitly or implicitly, include the notion
of purposeful activity in their comprehension of the concept are Park
and Burgess,[3] Bonney,[4] Dowd,[5] Young,[6] Pound,[7] Gillin and Gillin,[8] and
the author of the definition of social control given in the Dictionary
of Sociology.[9]

The twin criteria of usage and usefulness seem, in the writer's
opinion, to call for a limitation upon the extension of the concept
of social control so that it applies only to purposeful activity. First,
a concept which is broad enough to include the whole range of human
coexistence is of little value as a tool of analysis. Every contact of
human with human leaves its impress, exerts some influence, results in
some adjustment. To include all this in the range of activity to
which the concept applies, as Eubank and Bernard do, is to nullify

---

1. Lumley, op. cit., p. 13.
2. Ross, op. cit., p. viii.
3. Robert E. Park and Ernest W. Burgess, Introduction to the science of sociology, Chicago, The University of Chicago Press, 1921, pp. 785 ff.
4. Bonney, op. cit., p. x.
5. Dowd, op. cit., pp. 6, 11.
6. Kimball Young, Sociology, a study of society and culture, New York, American Book Company, 1942, p. 892.
7. Pound, op. cit., p. 16.
8. John L. Gillin and John P. Gillin, An introduction to sociology, New York, The Macmillan Company, 1942, p. 510.
9. "Social control," Dictionary of sociology, p. 279.

analysis. The same might be said, and Bain has said it, of the extension of the concept to all the socializing processes, with special emphasis upon those which are impersonal, non-purposive. The agencies of social control, in such a concept, are discovered on every conceivable level; they become synonymous with all the environmental factors in an individual's life. Lastly, the weight of usage is on the side of limiting the extension of the concept to the field of purposeful activity.

Social control as productive of social order.--The problem of social order, nomia, equilibrium, the uniformities, the "laws" of social behavior, is the central problem of sociology. It was Ross' consideration of this problem which led him to his study of social control. He put to himself the problem of determining to what extent social order is due to human nature and to what extent it is due to the "influence of social surroundings."[1] He concluded that it was due partly to both. The "influences of social surroundings" which are productive of social order were for Ross the limits of the extension of the concept of social control. Most authors have followed Ross in studying social control from this point of view. Therefore most of them, either explicitly or implicitly, make the concept comprehend those influences which make for order, discipline, uniformity, or conformity to group standards.[2] Conversely, students of social disorganization see it as

1. Ross, op. cit., p. viii.
2. Thus Park and Burgess, Hankins, Dowd, Landis, Pound, Gillin and Gillin, Young, in the works cited above; also, William F. Ogburn and Meyer F. Nimkoff, Sociology, Boston, Houghton and Mifflin Company, 1940, p. 265; and Robert L. Sutherland and Julian L. Woodward, Introductory sociology (2d ed.), Philadelphia, J. B. Lippincott Company, 1940, p. 800.

a breakdown in the functioning of social control.[1]

Lumley broke away from the Ross usage in extending the application of the concept of social control to any sort of "effective will-transference," even that of the tramp who cajoles a dollar from his victim. Eubank and Bernard, offering the narrowest comprehension and the broadest extension of the concept, make room for anti-social activity in their application. Bernard devotes a whole section of his work to "exploitive" social controls, including graft and fraud.[2] Bonney, who borrows a part of Park and Burgess' definition," an arbitrary interference in the social process,"[3] omits the qualifying phrase of the original which limits the extension of the concept to those interferences which are "supported by custom, law, and public opinion,"[4] i.e., the agencies of social order. Bain, as we have already seen, follows Lumley.

A certain latitude in the use of sociological concepts is generally permitted, even though deprecated. And there is no logical or etymological reason why the concept of social control should not extend to the dominating activities of organized crime as well as to those of the organized police. But again, the criteria of usefulness and usage must be applied. The concept of social control has been developed as an analytic tool in the study of the problem of social order, nomia, equilibrium, or whatever one chooses to call it. It seems to this author that the extension of the concept to activities which are

---

1. Cf. Ernest R. Mowrer, "Methodological problems in social disorganization," American sociological review, VI (1941), 839-849.
2. Bernard, op. cit., Part II, "The exploitive social controls," pp. 51-332.
3. Bonney, op. cit., p. x.
4. Park and Burgess, op. cit., p. 789.

deliberately disruptive of social order destroys the usefulness of the tool in the field for which it was originally designed. There is no corresponding gain in sight to compensate for this loss. And, once more, the preponderance of usage is on the other side.

The concept of social control, therefore, which would combine scientific usefulness with respect for usage, would include in its comprehension the elements of both purpose and social order.

One refinement is to be introduced in the concept as it will be used in this study. Since the expression "social order" suggests certain overtones of normative evaluation--witness the phrases "the new order", "the true social order", "a just social order"--and since even on a strictly empirical basis it is often difficult to determine when deviations are actually destructive of order, it seems better to think of the end product of social control as "conformity to group standards." In this connection, Linton's concept of "ideal patterns" proves useful. Ideal patterns are those "more or less conscious patterns of what the behavior of individuals in certain positions should be," which society uses as "guides to the training of these individuals."[1] This refinement is one of expression, rather than an actual modification of the concept. That the concept remains the same may be seen from Timasheff's convertible use of the terms:

> Behavior modeled on a pattern in force (i.e., on a
> socially supported pattern) is normal behavior...
> Normal behavior is coordinated behavior, for it is
> behavior in accordance with obligatory patterns.
> The process of imposing behavior patterns is social

---

1. Ralph Linton, The study of man, New York, D. Appleton-Century Co., 1936, p. 99. Cf. Clyde Kluckhohn, "The place of theory in anthropological studies," Philosophy of science, VI (1939), 338 f., for a criticism of the use of the concept "patterns."

coordination, and the result of coordination is
social order.[1]

It is the author's belief that the terminological change also reduces
the likelihood of committing the analysis to the theoretical implications which might be read into the expressions "social order",
"equilibrium", "nomia" and the like.

Definition.--In the study which follows, the concept of social
control will refer to conscious attempts to impose or enforce the ideal
patterns of society.

Pressure Groups

Social pressure.--Closely related to the concept of social control
is that of social pressure. So close, indeed, is the relationship
that one is at times used to define the other. Social control has been
defined as "the pressure upon each man...",[2] "those social pressures which
...",[3] "the pattern of pressure...."[4] On the other hand we find a
pressure group defined as "any group that endeavors to control the
policy...."[5]

MacIver has contributed an analysis which makes social pressure a
workable concept.[6] He distinguishes social pressures on the one hand
from those "direct authoritarian controls, effected through officials
or other accredited social agents and expressive of established codes";[7]
and on the other hand from the unorganized process of indoctrination

---

1. N. S. Timasheff, An introduction to the sociology of law, Cambridge,
   Harvard University Committee on Research in the social sciences,
   1939, p. 9.
2. Pound, op. cit., p. 18.
3. Gillin and Gillin, op. cit., p. 510.
4. Ogburn and Nimkoff, op. cit., p. 265.
5. Reuter, op. cit., p. 144.
6. R. M. MacIver, "Social pressures," Encyclopedia of the social
   sciences, XII, pp. 344-348.
7. Ibid., p. 344.

and habituation to which the established mores of every group subject its members.[1] Between these two he finds social pressures to be "socially created constraints which emanate from less sanctioned or less responsible sources," which are "informal and opportunistic in their operation," and "fluctuate incessantly in intensity and direction."[2]

Accepting this distinction, social pressures are a species of the genus which is social control. The conscious attempt to impose or enforce society's ideal patterns may proceed either through "direct authoritarian controls" or through constraints emanating from "less sanctioned and less responsible sources." Social pressures lack the individuating note which is the property of control exercised with authority. The distinction is not based on the identity of the agent who does the controlling. The state may, as Childs points out,[3] assume the role of a pressure group. When it does, however, it steps down from its pedestal of power; it invades a field wherein commands do not avail; it is noteworthy that pressure by the state usually employs the medium of propaganda, to bring pressure upon the human mind which is not amenable to authoritarian control.

Social pressures, as thus conceived by MacIver, are also marked off from the field of socialization of the personality, described previously. The note of conscious, deliberate purpose is implicit in MacIver's concept.

---

1. MacIver, op. cit., p. 345.
2. Ibid., p. 344.
3. Harwood L. Childs, The annals, CLXXIX (May, 1935), xi.

Pressure group.--When the concept of social pressure is used in connection with the group which exercises it, it popularly receives a broader comprehension, a narrower extension. In common parlance a pressure group is often taken to be "an organization whose main purpose is to have something done _for_ instead of _by_ a small minority."[1] Stuart Chase calls them the "Me First" groups.[2] Unfortunately Alfred McClung Lee has included this property in his tendentious definition of a pressure group:

> An actual or alleged group utilized by its leaders
> to force modifications in the policies of other
> groups or of a larger organization with which it is
> affiliated.... A pressure group usually concerns itself
> with the promotion of some aspect of "the general public
> interest," i.e., with obtaining special privileges for
> its leaders and members.[3]

For the sake of consistency and precision, the concept of pressure group in this study will be derived from the concept of social pressures as presented by MacIver. It will not comprehend the note of exploitation, hence it is applicable to a wider range of groups than is Lee's concept.

Briefly, a pressure group will be used in this study to mean _an organized group, lacking the direct control of authority, exercising socially created constraints upon the activities of an individual or of a group._

The Structure of Social Action

Because this is to be a study of a pressure group, and because pressure is a form of social action, the analysis will have to be

---

1. Francis A. Harding, "More blessed to get !", The American scholar, VIII (1938-1939), 35. Emphasis in original.
2. Stuart Chase, Democracy under pressure, New York, The Twentieth Century Fund, 1945, p. 133.
3. "Pressure group," Dictionary of sociology, pp. 134 f.

carried on within the framework of a conceptual scheme of the
structure of social action, explicitly or implicitly accepted. It is
better to be explicit.

The "means-end" schema.--Talcott Parsons, has isolated the
following analytic elements of the social act.

> (1) It implies an agent, an "actor." (2) For purposes
> of definition the act must have an "end," a future state
> of affairs toward which the process of action is
> oriented. (3) It must be initiated in a "situation"
> of which the trends of development differ in one or
> more important respects from the state of affairs to
> which the action is oriented, the end. This situation
> is in turn analyzable into two elements: those over which
> the actor has no control, that is which he cannot alter,
> or prevent from being altered, in conformity with his
> end, and those over which he has such control. The
> former may be termed the "conditions" of action, the
> latter the "means." Finally (4) there is inherent in the
> conception of this unit, in its analytical uses, a certain
> mode of relationship between these elements. That is, in
> the choice of alternative means to the end, in so far as
> the situation allows alternatives, there is a "normative
> orientation" of action.[1]

Objection.--Positivists do not like Parsons' schema. They do not
admit the empirical validity of the categories of means and ends.
Bierstedt, apropos of Parsons' analysis, wrote:

> The positivistic tradition,...requires as the very
> minimum criterion of a concept that it be reducible
> to referents which can directly be related to sense-
> experience or be reached by empirical operations.
> Ends and means by definition fail to satisfy this
> criterion. They are not sensory objects to which an
> investigator can respond. They do not express relations
> between objects which can be verified independently
> by other observers.[2]

---

1. Talcott Parsons, The structure of social action, New York, McGraw-
   Hill Book Company, Inc., 1937, p. 44.
2. Robert Bierstedt, "The means-end schema in sociological theory,"
   American sociological review, III (1938), 669.

Reason for adoption.--Epistemological discussion would take us far afield. A valid reason for accepting Parsons' schema can be placed on a very different level. All the students of social control, from Ross to Bernard, have given much attention to the "means of control." Lumley devoted his work exclusively to this phase of the subject. But it is impossible to speak of means without connoting ends; the terms are correlative. Hence the author is within the tradition of even the more positivistic sociologists in treating social control within the framework of the means-end schema. It would require extraordinary reasons to depart from this usage.

Accordingly this study of the Legion of Decency will proceed according to the following plan.

First, the Legion as a group, the agent or source of social pressure will be treated. Second, the values which constitute the end of the Legion's action will be analysed. Third, the means by which the Legion sought to reach its end will be studied. In this connection the conditions and the normative orientation of the Legion's action will be treated.

CHAPTER II

THE STRUCTURE OF THE LEGION OF DECENCY

Introduction

If one takes the pages of The New York Times as an indicator of
the American public's awareness of those social activities which are
national in scope, one is led to conclude that the Legion of Decency
burst in upon the American consciousness with a sharp impact, early
in June, 1934.

From the beginning of the year, up to that month, the Times had
printed only nine items relating to motion picture standards of
morality. But in June there were twenty-five such items; in July
there were fifty-eight; by the end of the year the total had mounted
to one hundred and thirty-eight. Almost every one of these was
concerned with the Legion of Decency. At first the reports related
localized activities; but very soon the readers of the Times were
aware that a nation-wide campaign was in progress.

Who had started the Legion of Decency? The Times did not seem
to know. Toward the end of June it reported: "It was learned in Rome
that the campaign was undertaken without specific instructions from
the Vatican, nor has the Pope taken part in it."[1] Had this pressure
group formed spontaneously? Through what process had it emerged upon
the scene?

Who were, and who are the members of the Legion? Is it true

1. The New York times, June 26, 1934.

that the Legion is "a small reactionary group in the Catholic Church?"[1]
What proportion of Catholics signed the pledge of membership? Is the
membership exclusively Catholic?

Is the Legion of Decency really an organization? When the Civil
Liberties Union addressed an open letter to the Legion a Catholic
journal commented:

> Just who is supposed to answer this letter it does
> not make clear. It seems to harbor the notion that
> the Legion is a society like itself, with officers,
> dues and by-laws. But the Legion is merely several
> million Americans who have signed a pledge binding
> themselves to stay away from immoral movies. The
> Legion is a movement, not an organized body.[2]

Is there any organization to the Legion? If there is, what is its
structure?

These questions are to be answered in the course of the following
analysis of the structure of the Legion of Decency.

Structure is "a relatively permanent or persistent organization
of parts."[3] Closely correlated to the concept of structure is that
of function, "the type or types of action of which a structure is
distinctively capable."[4] In a sense, "structure is function and
function is structure."[5] The analysis of structure, accordingly, is
less a matter of charts and blueprints than a study of functional
differentiation.

This chapter, therefore, will describe the functions of the various

---

1. Morris L. Ernst and Alexander Lindey, The censor marches on, New
   York, Doubleday, Doran and Company, 1940, p. 216.
2. America, LI (October 6, 1934), 602.
3. Hornell Hart, "Structure," Dictionary of sociology, p. 310.
4. Hart, "Function," ibid., p. 125.
5. Charles E. Merriam, Public and private government, New Haven, Yale
   University Press, 1944, p. 56. Cf. Grace L. Coyle, Social process
   in organized groups, New York, John Wiley and Sons, 1932, pp. 94 ff.;
   B. Warren Brown, Social groups, Chicago, The Fairthorn Company, 1926,
   pp. 63 ff.

parts of the pressure group. To some extent this will introduce
factual material which may seem to belong more properly to the study
of the "means" adopted by the Legion. Here, however, the emphasis
will be directed exclusively to the functions as indicators of
organizational structure.

Structure, insofar as it involves function, is active, dynamic.
It emerges as the group emerges, takes shape as the group assumes an
articulated form, becomes fixed only if and when the group becomes
a permanent entity. Accordingly, the structural analysis of the
Legion of Decency is to be divided into sections which parallel the
stages of group development: (1) the process of emergence of the group,
(2) the process of formation of the group, and (3) the permanent
organization of the group.

Chronology

The following summary of the stages of development may serve to
put the subsequent analysis in a clear temporal frame of reference.

1. The process of emergence of the Legion of Decency began
back in the Winter of 1929-1930, when the motion picture industry
agreed to make its product in conformity with a code of moral
standards, generally called the Production Code. The process continued
during the next three years in the course of which certain attempts
were made to create social pressure for conformity with the Code. It
came to an end in November, 1933, when the Catholic Bishops appointed
a committee to plan and conduct a campaign against immoral movies.

2. The process of formation lasted from November, 1933 to
November, 1934. During this time an articulated structure made its

appearance, a differentiation of function marking off the activities of the committee, local episcopal leaders, and member-followers.

3. In November, 1934, the Legion became a permanent group. The permanent features of its structure have remained substantially unchanged up to the present.

The Process of Emergence[1]

The Legion of Decency movement may seem to the casual observer to have caught fire with something that looks like spontaneous combustion. But closer examination into its origins shows much previous conscious social activity.

There are clues pointing in the direction of this conclusion in two features observed during the formative process. The first of these is that the Legion activity was directed and principally located within the membership of the Catholic Church. The second is the fact that the Episcopal Committee was so ready to give speedy approval to the industry's promise to provide effective regulation of its product according to the provisions of the production code. This callida junctura of the Catholic Church and the Production Code points to previous spade-work.

If there is some one event prior to the origin of the Legion which contains within itself the germ of these two features, it may be

----

1. The information upon which this section is based has been derived, where not otherwise indicated, from study of the private files of Martin Quigley, the Reverend Wilfrid Parsons, S.J., and of the editor's files of America; from interviews with Archbishop John T. McNicholas, Quigley, and Fathers Parsons, Lord and Dinneen; and from communications from Fathers Lord and Parsons, Quigley and Breen.

considered to be "crucial"[1] for the process of the Legion's emergence.
Furthermore, if genetic explanation for the emergence of the Legion
need go back no further than this event, it may be considered to be
the initial event of the series. This does not mean that the crucial,
initial event is the cause of the final emergence of the Legion, in
the way that the first link in a causal chain is the cause of the
last.[2] The event is to be considered crucial and initial insofar as
it satisfies the quest for that type of understanding of social
phenomena which only the genetic explanation can give.

In this sense it may be said that the process which ended with
the emergence of the Legion began with the introduction of the
Production Code into the motion picture industry's nascent system
of self-regulation.

The Production Code[3]

The concept of a code of moral standards which should regulate
the output of the motion picture producers of Hollywood originated in
1929 with Martin Quigley.[4]

---

1. R. M. MacIver, Social causation, Boston, Ginn and Company, 1942,
   p. 186, uses the term "crucial event" to indicate the "precipitant
   overthrowing the prior operative system."
2. Cf. ibid., pp. 184 ff.
3. "A code to govern the making of talking, synchronized and silent
   motion pictures, formulated by Association of Motion Picture Producers,
   Inc., and The Motion Picture Producers and Distributors of America,
   Inc.," n.d., mimeographed. The M.P.P.D.A. has distributed printed
   copies of the Code under the titles: (1) "A code to maintain social
   and community values in the production of silent, synchronized and
   talking motion pictures," n.d., and (2) "Production code and uniform
   interpretation," n.d. The Code and its accompanying "Resolution for
   uniform interpretation," with amendments to date, may be found in
   International motion picture almanac, 1944-45, pp. 695-703. The
   M.P.P.D.A. is preparing to issue an up-to-date printing of the Code
   with amendments.
4. On the difference between the "Don'ts" and "Be carefuls" of 1927, and
   the Production code, see Chapter IV, pp.

Quigley is the publisher of influential motion picture trade
journals.[1] The attitude of the Quigley publications toward the moral
quality of the movies has been consistent since 1915.

> There is a most intimate relation between the
> maintenance of an acceptable moral standard in
> photoplay production and the commercial prosperity
> of the motion picture industry.[2]

His editorial policy has opposed censorship, which is costly to the
industry; at the same time it has insisted that films be "clean and
wholesome to the last detail."[3]

Censorship forces had been very active in Chicago, where Quigley's
publishing business was then located, ever since that city's
ordinance of 1907. Prominent among them was the Reverend F. G.
Dinneen, S.J. He and Quigley had been members for some years of a
Commission on Motion Picture Censorship appointed by the mayor of
Chicago. In the late summer of 1929, a particularly tense situation
had arisen in Chicago, with the censorship forces and the representatives of the film industry locked in stubborn struggle. Father
Dinneen was prominent in the conflict. Quigley was in New York at
the time, but was kept informed of developments in Chicago.

Quigley's reflections on the situation brought him to the
conception of a project which he thought could achieve the objectives

---

1. O. W. Riegel, "Nationalism in press, radio and cinema," American
   sociological review, III (1938), 513, refers to Quigley together
   with the Hays office as "the spokesmen" for the motion picture
   industry.
2. Exhibitors' herald, Spetember 30, 1916, p. 10.
3. Exhibitors' film exchange, August 31, 1915, p. 18. This was one
   month after Quigley became editor of the publication. For similar
   quotations, see Exhibitors' film exchange, September 18, 1915, p. 8,
   October 30, 1915, p. 10; Exhibitors' herald, September 23, 1916,
   p. 9, September 30, 1916, p. 9, January 26, 1918, p. 11; Motion
   picture herald, passim.

of the censorship group without incurring the costs and other liabilities which made censorship so objectionable to the film industry. His plan was to offer the industry an integrated code of generally accepted moral standards to guide the producers in the making of films which would not run afoul of censorship and other protesting groups.

On his return to Chicago, Quigley outlined his proposal to Father Dinneen. Father Dinneen was persuaded that the project had merit; he suggested that Father Daniel A. Lord, S.J. be engaged to assist in drawing up the proposed code. Father Lord, a former pupil and a close friend of Father Dinneen, had been in Hollywood not long before as technical adviser in the production of the religious film, "The King of Kings."

Father Lord, after conferences with Quigley, put into writing their statement of the relevant moral principles and the application of them to the production of motion pictures.

Quigley brought his proposal to the attention of Will Hays, who arranged that Quigley have the opportunity of presenting it to the film producers at a special meeting in Hollywood. After some sessions with the producers, Quigley asked Father Lord to come to Hollywood to urge the producers to accept the code plan. Father Lord's efforts were successful; the producers accepted the code substantially as it had been offered to them. Most of the provisions of the "Don'ts" and "Be Carefuls" were added to the text that Father Lord had originally written; the format was revised, and there were slight textual alterations. This code, ever since known as the Production Code, was given final ratification by the Motion Picture Producers and Distributors of America, Inc., under the date of

March 31, 1930.

The conception, formulation and acceptance of the Production Code was the initial, crucial event in the process of emergence of the Legion of Decency.

With the acceptance of the Code, the process entered a new phase.

Pressure from Individual Ethical Leadership

The film industry had committed itself to the provisions of the Code. But would the producers abide by that commitment? How could conformity to Code standards be assured? The Reverend Wilfrid Parsons, S.J., editor of the Catholic national weekly, America, raised this question in an article on the Code written just after its ratification. His answer is significant for future developments.

> What about its enforcement?... No form of outside force except that of public opinion is feasible or desirable, and no form of censorship except self-censorship will work in practice. The producers have given hostages to public opinion by the very publication of the Code.[1]

Public opinion, it developed, was to be represented by ethical leaders[2] who would exert pressure on the industry for conformity to the Code. "What we must do, it seems to me, is to create in the industry's minds an impression that influential people expect the Code to be obeyed; if that happens it will be obeyed."[3]

---

1. "A code for motion pictures," America, XLIII (April 19, 1930), 33.
2. Timasheff, Sociology of law, p. 89: "Persons whose recognition of ethical rules is decisive for the attitude of others may be called 'ethical leaders'." Cf. Ross, Social control, p. 363.
3. Wilfrid Parsons, S.J. to Cardinal Hayes, July 17, 1930.

The protagonists in the activity of enlisting the support of ethical leaders were Quigley, Father Lord, Father Dinneen, Father Parsons, Joseph I. Breen, and, towards the end of the period, Monsignor Joseph M. Corrigan.[1]

Joseph I. Breen had become interested in the Code through his personal acquaintance with Martin Quigley. Breen had come to Chicago to direct public relations for the Eucharistic Congress held there in 1925. He had returned to that city some two years before the Code was projected, taking a position first with the Chicago World's Fair of 1933 organization and then with the Peabody Coal Company. After the Code had been accepted, his interest in it led him to work for some months with Quigley in the effort to get the Code known and approved by ethical leaders.

Father Parsons had known Breen for years; they had corresponded intermittently. Through Breen, Father Parsons first heard of the Code project. In the middle of March, 1930, he wrote to his fellow-Jesuit, Father Lord, about the Code, expressing his intention to "get behind it" vigorously.[2] A few days after this he attended a luncheon in New York, at which the Hays office made a preliminary announcement of the Code to the people connected with its Public Relations Department. Within a week Father Parsons was in Chicago, meeting with Quigley, Breen, Father Lord and Father Dinneen, planning with them ways and means of creating pressure on behalf of the Code.

1. The late Bishop and Rector of the Catholic University of America.
2. Wilfrid Parsons, S.J. to Daniel A. Lord, S.J., March 15, 1930.

Thereafter he was active in the process, writing of the Code in the pages of America, participating in the correspondence and discussion which mark this period.

Much of the Quigley-Breen effort was directed towards editors of the Catholic press. An instance of the range of this activity is an article which appeared in the Vatican City daily, in praise of the Code: "...il codice e del tutto consono ai principii della morale cristiana, e quindi alla morale naturale che e confermata e illuminata della dottrina cattolica."[1] This article was brought to the attention of Will Hays as "an encouraging endorsement of the Code idea."[2]

Through Father Dinneen, the Archbishop of Chicago, Cardinal Mundelein, had become interested in the Code even before its acceptance by the industry. Father Dinneen's efforts to obtain the Cardinal's public approval of the Code were complicated by the local censorship problem in Chicago. However, within a few months America printed his endorsement of the Code, together with a similar statement obtained by Father Parsons from Cardinal Hayes, the Archbishop of New York.[3]

But despite these and other scattered successes, the endeavor to create pressure through individual ethical leaders was not notably effective. Eight months after the Code's ratification, Father Parsons wrote:

> It is a curious commentary on our civilization that the Code passed almost unnoticed by the public at large... With certain exceptions Catholic leaders have been conspicuously silent and ineffective.[4]

---

1. L'osservatore Romano, 27-28, Luglio, 1931.
2. Martin Quigley to Will H. Hays, August 14, 1931.
3. Wilfrid Parsons,"Motion picture morality," America, XLIV (November 15, 1930), 131-133.
4. Ibid., 131 f.

Martin Quigley, writing several years later, recalled that "Despite the recent worldwide recognition of the moral potency of the screen the problem was one that only dawned tardily on the consciousness of important moral leadership."[1]

The significance for the emergence of the Legion of Decency of this unsuccessful attempt lies in the fact that it laid the ground for the decision to seek the support of institutionally organized ethical leadership.

Pressure from Institutional Ethical Leadership

The decision to seek the support of the organization of Catholic Bishops was the product of a period of reflection, discussion and communication.[2] During this period, Quigley moved to New York, where his contact with Father Parsons became frequent. Breen, who became Assistant to the President in the Hays office in 1931, moved to Hollywood in January, 1932. These three met at frequent intervals, often in the company of Monsignor Corrigan.

At one of these sessions, in September, 1933, Monsignor Corrigan suggested that it would help their cause if the Most Reverend Amleto Giovanni Cicognani, newly arrived Apostolic Delegate in the United States, should make a public pronouncement on the motion picture problem. A few weeks later, through Monsignor Corrigan's instrumentality, Archbishop Cicognani, in his first public address in the

1. Martin Quigley, Decency in motion pictures, New York The Macmillan Company, 1937, p. 24.
2. Correspondence was frequent and lengthy. The files of Father Parsons and of Martin Quigley contain sixty-two letters on these matters, exchanged among themselves, Father Dinneen, Father Lord, and Joseph I. Breen, during the years 1930-1933. There are many references to other letters which have not been preserved. Father Parsons recalls innumerable telephone conversations, four or five a week, between himself and Quigley during this period and during the campaign.

United States, concluded an indictment of the morals of the movies with the words:

> Catholics are called by God, the Pope, the Bishops and the priests to a united and vigorous campaign for the purification of the cinema, which has become a deadly menace to morals.[1]

There can be no doubt that the words of the Apostolic Delegate influenced the Catholic Bishops to take action six weeks later.

They were not the sole determining factor, however. The process of enlisting the support of the organized hierarchy had begun some time before. Father Dinneen had received such a suggestion from Cardinal Mundelein, according to which Father Lord would describe the problem to the Bishops at their annual meeting.[2] Concurrently, in California, the Most Reverend John J. Cantwell, then Bishop, now Archbishop of the territory which includes Hollywood, was coming to a similar decision. He had discussed the Code situation with Breen in California. He did not favor the tactic of creating pressure for the Code through public statements made by ethical leaders. He favored more direct action. Breen wrote to Father Parsons, "He has set himself to do whatever he can to cope with the wrong kind of screen fare--and he has fire in his eye."[3] In the event, it was Bishop Cantwell who presented the situation to the Bishops at their annual meeting in November, 1933.

At this meeting the Bishops condemned immorality in the films, demanded that the industry reform, sanctioned a national campaign to

---

1. The New York times, October 2, 1933.
2. F. G. Dinneen, S.J. to Wilfrid Parsons, S.J., July 12, 1933.
3. Joseph I. Breen to Wilfrid Parsons, S.J., August 11, 1933.

effect this reform, and appointed an Episcopal Committee on Motion Pictures to plan, control and conduct the campaign.[1]

So ended the process of emergence begun four years before.

The foregoing account of that process has made it clear that behind the apparent spontaneity of the Legion of Decency campaign was the conscious activity of a few men, who labored, first, to provide a solution for the problem of movie morals, and then to provide pressure to make the solution work. Self-regulation of the film industry in conformity with the Production Code was the solution. The pressure was to come from the activity of institutional ethical leadership, the organization of Catholic Bishops. Thus it was no accident that the Legion of Decency was directed and principally located within the Catholic Church; and it was not by chance that the Episcopal Committee directed the pressure of the Legion toward supporting the film industry's system of self-regulation according to the Production Code.

The process of formation of the Legion of Decency began with the appointment of the Episcopal Committee. The structure which took shape during the process is now to be studied.

----

1. The members of the Committee were: The Most Reverend John T. McNicholas, Archbishop of Cincinnati, chairman; the Most Reverend John J. Cantwell, Bishop of Los Angeles and San Diego; the Most Reverend John F. Noll, Bishop of Fort Wayne, and the Most Reverend Hugh C. Boyle, Bishop of Pittsburgh. Bishop Boyle resigned in 1942; the Most Reverend Francis P. Keough, Bishop of Providence, was then appointed to the Committee. In 1943, Archbishop McNicholas resigned, and Bishop Keough was elected Chairman; the Most Reverend Joseph H. Albers, Bishop of Lansing, was appointed to the Committee. In 1944, the Most Reverend Bryan J. McEntegart, Bishop of Ogdensburg, was appointed to the Committee.

The Process of Formation

The appointment of an Episcopal Committee on Motion Pictures introduced the institutional ethical leadership of the Catholic Bishops into the problem field of motion picture morals.

The success of the Legion of Decency, which the Episcopal Committee created five months after its appointment, is to some extent attributable to the fact that it is sustained and directed by the organized Hierarchy of the Catholic Church. Indeed, the author has been assured by interested non-Catholics that it was solely the organization of the Church which "turned the trick" after so many earlier protests had failed. Thorp emphasizes the Church's "genius for organization."[1] Goldstein says, "Neither the Protestant nor the Jewish groups possess similar organization or discipline and, therefore, could not hope to achieve a similar result."[2]

The structure of the Bishops' organization which sponsored the Legion of Decency demands close consideration if the structural development of the Legion itself is to be understood.

The Hierarchical Structure

Judgments such as those just quoted are apt to reflect a common misapprehension which conceives the Catholic Church to be organized along military lines: a rigidly vertical organization in which there is but one central repository of power. In this conception, some one person, probably the Pope,[3] issues a command, and delegated officials

---

1. Margaret F. Thorp, America at the movies, New Haven, Yale University Press, 1939, p. 203.
2. Sidney E. Goldstein, "The motion pictures and social control," The movies on trial, ed. by William J. Perlman, New York, The Macmillan Company, 1936, p. 224.
3. Cf. The New York times, June 26, 1934.

hasten to set in motion the machinery by which well-disciplined underlings carry out the orders. Such a view of the Church's structure is uninformed.

Papal and episcopal power.--The Roman Catholic Church is organized throughout the world on a twofold basis. One structural base is the power residing in the papacy. The other is the power residing in the episcopacy. The structure of the Church, relative to papal power, is vertical. Relative to episcopal power it is horizontal.

The papacy is recognized as having, in its own right, final authority in matters of faith and morals.

> This jurisdiction is universal, extending over both clergy and laity...it is immediate, in that the Pope may deal directly with any members of the Church; it is sovereign because all in the Church are subordinate to him and he to none--in a word, he is the bishop of bishops, of the hierarchy as well as of the faithful.[1]

On the other hand, the same kind and degree of power is exercised by the episcopacy when it meets as a collective body in the sessions of an Ecumenical Council. Furthermore, individual bishops exercise direct power over the faithful of their dioceses, not in virtue of authority delegated to them by the Pope, but in virtue of their position as recognized successors of the Apostles, who, Catholics maintain, were given a direct mandate by the Founder of their Church.

> ...the power of each bishop over his diocese, the right to govern it, is a direct power which the Pope cannot suppress, or reduce to too narrow limits.[2]

1. Michael Williams, The Catholic Church in action, New York, The Macmillan Company, 1934, p. 188.
2. Ibid., p. 189.

Apart from his subjection to the laws of Ecumenical, Plenary and Provincial Councils,[1] each Bishop is autonomous in respect to every other Bishop except the Bishop of Rome, the Pope. This autonomy is so complete that, up to 1917, there had been no permanent machinery in the United States for concerted action by the Bishops.

The National Catholic Welfare Conference.--To meet the problems raised by the first World War, the National Catholic War Council was organized. The Bishops' explanation of the new organization reads in part:

> The oldtime adjustments of our national life have
> been changed by the war. The pathways along which
> our energies have gone in the past have had to be
> recharted;...The Church must face consciously the
> overwhelming problems of morality and spiritual
> reinforcement in the camp, in the community and on
> the battle-line.... In the nature of the case,
> duplication, delay, oversight and waste are forbidden.
> ... The National Catholic War Council was created,
> therefore, because these needs were apparent.[2]

After the War, "convinced of the need for a similar agency for peacetime purposes," the Bishops voted to maintain themselves in a permanent association which was later named the National Catholic Welfare Conference.[3]

The Conference "has not and never can have any mandatory or legislative power. Nothing can be done in a diocese except by

1. An Ecumenical Council includes all the bishops of the Church; a Plenary Council includes the bishops of several Provinces; a Provincial Council includes the bishops of one Province. These Councils are legislative; their decisions are mandatory. There have been Plenary Councils in the United States in 1852, 1866 and 1884. Provincial Councils meet every twenty years.
2. Handbook of the National Catholic War Council, Washington, D.C., 1918, pp. 30-33.
3. The National Catholic Welfare Conference, Washington, D.C., n.d., p. 3.

permission of the Ordinary."[1] Bishops, free to join the Conference or
not, are free to accept or reject the recommendations made by the
Conference or any agency created by it. The episcopacy of the Catholic
Church in the United States is not vertically organized.

The coordination of episcopal efforts achieved through the
Conference is not the result of subordination of individual power
centers to one superior center; there is none such in the United
States. Uniformity of action resulting from the Conference is not,
then, an imposed uniformity.[2] Unless it be a natural uniformity,
traceable to "the inherent tendency of different individuals to react
in the same way to the same stimuli,"[3] concerted action by the members
of the Conference must be the result of imitation of the action
patterns set forth by the Conference or one of its sub-sections or
Committees.

In the case of the Legion of Decency, the Bishops exhibited such
a uniformity of response as is not found in natural uniformities; all
but six of over one hundred Bishops reported activity in the Legion
campaign.

---

1. The National Catholic Welfare Conference, p. 8; cf. Amleto Giovanni
   Cicognani, Canon law, trans. Joseph M. O'Hara and Francis Brennan,
   Philadelphia, The Dolphin Press, 1934, p. 97, n. 82: "Rightly must
   Plenary and Provincial Councils be distinguished from the meetings
   of the various Bishops of a certain nation, or of a particular
   territory.... Such assemblies of Bishops are vested with no
   legislative power,...."
2. Timasheff, Sociology of law, p. 8: "The third class of uniformities
   is formed by sets of similar acts within which a certain behavior
   is 'imposed' on group-members as an obligatory pattern for their
   behavior."
3. Brown, Social groups, pp. 38 f.; cf. Timasheff, op. cit., pp. 7 f.

The uniformity of episcopal action on the Legion of Decency has no other explanation than that the Bishops accepted both the moral values which were the goal of Legion activity and the means-pattern proposed by the Episcopal Committee.

If this analysis is not at fault, the strength of the Legion of Decency must not be attributed exclusively, nor even principally, to the structural form of its organization. "Genius for organization" was secondary. The primary factor was the unity of moral viewpoint which led the Bishops to coordinate their activities along uniform line.

The Episcopal Committee on Motion Pictures

The National Catholic Welfare Conference is directed by an Administrative Board of ten Archbishops and Bishops. This Board includes the Episcopal Chairmen of the eight permanent Departments of the Conference. Special Episcopal Committees, appointed by the General Assembly of the Bishops for particular or for temporary functions, work in conjunction with the Administrative Board, to which their reports are referred.

The Episcopal Committee on Motion Pictures is one of these special committees, appointed for the particular purpose of planning and conducting a campaign to effect reform in the motion picture industry.

As an agency of the Conference, the Committee can recommend, but not make mandatory, acceptance of its policies and plans by the individual Bishops.

The structural autonomy of the individual Bishops was evidenced during the first few months of the Committee's existence, when it solicited and received suggestions from the member Bishops of the Conference. It is evidenced, too, in the wording of the Committee's communications to the Bishops. For example, the letter which accompanied the copy of the pledge formula sent to all the Bishops said, "You may think it well to prepare a Pledge for your diocese or to authorize some one to do so. You may use the enclosed in any way that you wish."[1] Never did the Episcopal Committee use the imperative in the few communications it issued to the Bishops.

Structurally important, too, for continuity with the previous process of emergence, is the fact that during the first period of its activities, and later, the Committee did not ignore the initiators of the pressure movement, Quigley, et. al.

Early in March, Archbishop McNicholas, chairman of the Committee, wrote to Father Dinneen, asking for his suggestions. Father Dinneen asked Father Parsons, and Quigley for their advice, conferred with Archbishop McNicholas, and reported back to the others. In this same month, Quigley and Breen conferred with Bishop Cantwell, who was on the Committee. In April, Quigley went to Cincinnati at the invitation of Archbishop McNicholas.

Breen's position in the reorganized Production Code Administration removed him for further activity in the affairs of the Legion of Decency after June. Father Dinneen was intensely active throughout the campaign in Chicago; he was also officially a member of the National Committee of Priests appointed in June; but this Committee was little

---

1. "Report of the Episcopal Committee on Motion Pictures," (unpublished), Washington, D.C., 1935, p. 4. Hereafter referred to as "Report."

heard from thereafter. Father Lord contributed to the campaign as an active pamphleteer and publicist, and Father Parsons gave many columns of _America_ to the Legion; neither had any official or direct connection with the Episcopal Committee.

Quigley and Monsignor Corrigan, more than any of the other initiators, were in direct contact with Archbishop McNicholas. Quigley and Archbishop McNicholas formed something of a structural axis, around which all other advisers on policy circulated in irregular orbits. Quigley's special contribution was his long experience of direct knowledge and contact with men and affairs within the film industry. It may be surmised, too, that since he had fathered the Code, he had a paternal eagerness to make a large sacrifice of time and money to get for it the support it needed to be a success.

This survival and integration of the original promoters for pressure on behalf of the Code was conditioned upon the readiness of the Episcopal Committee to make use of them; even more it was conditioned upon the readiness of these men to abandon their role of initiators of policy and to give their individual support to the new policy-making group. The latter process was facilitated by the fact that the earlier group was unorganized and so less apt to be dominated by concern for the preservation of group identity and independence of activity.

In the structural pattern, the Episcopal Committee quickly took the position of the makers of policy. But theirs was not a power position in relation to the individual Bishops who carried on the localized activities of the Legion. Nor was their activity an abrupt break with the policies of the past. Of the Episcopal Committee's place in the structure of the Legion it may be said, "It is not the authority _per se_ or the hierarchy _per se_ but the role planned, the contribution or the service rendered that gives it importance and recognition."[1]

Local Bishops

The press came late upon the news that a nation-wide Legion of Decency campaign was in progress because the announcement of the plan to recruit a Legion of Decency, made on April 11, 1934, was communicated directly and separately to the Bishops of each of the one hundred and four dioceses of the Catholic Church in the United States.

The primary function of the local Bishops, as implied in the announcement, was to recruit pledged followers of the Legion. The organization of the campaign to secure pledged members was to be a decentralized activity, conducted separately in each diocese.

No new organization on the local level had to be constructed for this campaign. The ordinary channels of communication available to Catholic Bishops sufficed. There were pastoral letters from the Bishop read in all the churches of his diocese. There were letters to the clergy instructing them to preach on the moral ills of the movies, urging the signing of the pledge. There were editorials, articles and news items in the diocesan newspapers, and sometimes in the secular press. There were addresses on local radio stations, and at the gatherings of the numerous religious and social organizations

---

1. Merriam, _Public and private government_, p. 55.

of the laity which abound in each diocese. In all of this activity
the only expense incurred was the bill for printing the pledges.

This ready-made local organization was supplemented, and to a
certain degree coordinated by the national press service of the
National Catholic Welfare Conference, which provided the local Catholic
press with news of activities in other areas.

But to an extraordinary degree the local campaigns proceeded independently of each other. Each chose its own time to begin recruiting.
Some did not begin until late in the year, while a very few had anti-
cipated the announcement of the Episcopal Committee and had already
gathered similar pledges on their own initiative. Each adopted its
own technique. Some held mass-meetings and public demonstrations,
while others adopted a quieter tone. Each had its own tempo. Some
did all the recruiting on one day, while others proceeded at a more
gradual pace.

The secondary function of the local Bishops was to exert pressure
through protests to local exhibitors. As will be seen, the means most
favored was a personal letter from the Bishop to the exhibitor. But
there are instances, in a few dioceses, of organized demonstrations
and of calls upon exhibitors made by protesting delegations. In the
exercise of this function, as in that of recruiting, there was no
uniform pattern of activity.

The Followers

The individual member who signed or recited the pledge of the
Legion of Decency assumed the discharge of one function: that of
refusing to patronize morally objectionable films. By doing this he

made his contribution to the sum total of pressure exerted against the movie industry.

To fulfill this function there was no need for structural differentiation among the members. They were all doing the same thing, proceeding independently along parallel lines. Brown has made the observation,

> If each member bore the same relation to the central objective, little structure would be necessary. In a section gang, each man does about the same work with his pick and shovel and crowbar, just as in a schoolroom each student has identical tasks, making internal structure unnecessary.[1]

Nor was there need for structure to maintain the existence of the Legion of Decency. The pre-existent diocesan organization provided the machinery for recruiting the members, and for maintaining future contact among them. There was no need for officers, for meetings, for local headquarters, nor for dues to pay the expenses of these.

As far as the pledged followers were concerned, it was an accurate description of structure to assert that the Legion was "merely several million Americans who have signed a pledge binding themselves to stay away from immoral movies." It was true of them that they formed a "movement, not an organized body."[2]

Number of Catholic pledges.--There has been no official statement of the precise number of Catholics pledged to the Legion of

---

1. Brown, op. cit., p. 68.
2. America, LI (October 6, 1934), 602.

Decency in 1934. The Episcopal Committee's "Report" says
cautiously, "It has been difficult to estimate the number of pledges
signed throughout the United States. Some place the number at more
than 5,000,000."[1]

The reason for this situation is to be found in the decentralized
structure of the recruiting movement. In some dioceses the signed
pledges were returned to the Bishop's office and tabulated there. In
other dioceses the pastors of the local churches kept the signed
pledges and made no report to their Bishops of the number of members
thus recruited. In still others, apparently, the pledge was only
orally administered.

Ninety-eight dioceses reported upon their campaigns to the
Episcopal Committee; of these only thirty-two reported the number of
those who signed the pledge. Many of these figures are not final or
complete. Most of them are clearly not precise. Some include school
children, others are exclusively adults; some include upper grade
school children, but not those in the lower grades; one diocese notes
that many of the pledges represent whole families; another notes that
only the pledges of school children were tabulated. Most of the
figures are submitted without explanation. However, these figures
are the only reasonably reliable source from which the total Catholic
membership can be estimated. An estimate based on such incomplete
and unsatisfactory data, will, of course, be no more accurate or precise
than the sources upon which it relies.

---

1. "Report," p. 4.

The Catholic population of the United States in 1934 was reported by the Catholic Directory to be 20,322,594.[1] The thirty-two dioceses reporting the number of signed pledges had a total Catholic population, according to the same source, of 7,615,765. They reported a total of 3,110,454 signed pledges; 40.8% of the Catholic population of their dioceses.

It is most improbable that the reported figures represent nearly all the members ever recruited. Such a conclusion would be based upon the assumption that the dioceses which reported no figures obtained no members. But many of the reports, without giving precise figures, speak of "large numbers," or report thousands of pledges distributed to parishes but not returned to a central tabulating office. And some of the dioceses where it is known that activity in the Legion was very intense, such as Detroit and Boston, are not represented in the report.

It is more reasonable to take the dioceses which reported as sufficiently representative for statistical calculation, and to attempt to find the probable limits within which the actual total is to be found. Table 1 presents the figures. With 95% probability, the number of Catholic pledges obtained lies somewhere within the fiducial limits of 7,000,000 and 9,000,000. Considering the nature of the data, it would be unsound procedure to try to be more precise than this.

In any case, the number is sufficiently large to make untenable the proposition that the Legion is a "small reactionary group in the Catholic Church."[2] Moreover, Legion followers were not limited to the

---

1. All baptized Catholics, regardless of age, are included in this figure. It is not an accurate figure; generally it is considered that the true total is somewhat higher.
2. Ernst and Lindey, op. cit., p. 216.

TABLE 1

SIGNED PLEDGES REPORTED BY 32 DIOCESES, 1934

Diocese	Catholic Population	Pledges Reported	Percent of Population Pledged
Alexandria, La.	50,000	7,000	14.0
Belleville, Ill.	71,800	24,792	34.5
Boise, Idaho	19,273	10,000	51.9
Brooklyn, N.Y.	1,086,722	300,000	27.6
Buffalo, N.Y.	334,115	75,000	22.4
Chicago, Ill.	1,159,390	800,000	69.0
Cleveland, Ohio	548,403	300,000	54.7
Dubuque, Iowa	118,920	48,000	40.4
Duluth, Minn.	65,744	15,000	22.8
El Paso, Texas	109,110	30,000	27.5
Fall River, Mass.	178,372	65,000	36.4
Ft. Wayne, Ind.	167,780	60,000	35.7
Great Falls, Mont.	31,488	18,000	57.1
Indianapolis, Ind.	127,772	59,000	46.2
La Crosse, Wis.	126,653	50,000	39.5
Leavenworth, Kan.	79,004	50,000	63.3
Milwaukee, Wis.	350,000	200,000	57.2
Monterey-Fresno, Cal.	62,917	8,661	13.8
Ogdensburg, N.Y.	107,646	55,000	51.1
Philadelphia, Pa.	823,050	300,000	36.5
Pittsburg, Pa.	585,289	70,548	12.1
Raleigh, N.C.	9,102	5,000	54.9
Richmond, Va.	37,069	8,000	21.6
Rochester, N.Y.	218,400	70,000	32.1
St. Paul, Minn.	281,676	100,000	35.5
Santa Fe, N.M.	139,473	100,000	71.6
Scranton, Pa.	328,655	130,000	39.6
Syracuse, N.Y.	201,161	75,000	37.3
Spokane, Wash.	29,275	5,632	19.2
Wheeling, W. Va.	64,247	3,221	5.0
Wilmington, Del.	34,189	16,000	46.8
Winona, Minn.	68,600	51,600	75.0
TOTAL	7,615,765	3,110,454	40.8

$\overline{X}$: 17.95
$\sigma_{\overline{x}}$: 3.15 (standard error of mean)
σ : 2.24 (standard error of standard deviation)
95% fiducial limits: 6,848,714 and 9,368,716
Source: "Report of the Episcopal Committee on motion pictures," Catholic
Directory, 1934, pp. 331-376.

Catholics who signed the pledge.

Number of non-Catholic pledges.--The cooperation of Protestant
and Jewish clergymen, and of non-sectarian organizations in securing
signed pledges was welcomed by the Catholic leaders. While there is
no evidence of the extent of the non-sectarian activity, there is ample
indication of extensive religious support for the Legion from groups
other than the Catholic.

Forty-one of the diocesan reports to the Episcopal Committee
make explicit mention of Protestant and Jewish activities in support
of the Legion. One Bishop reported, "Within the writer's own diocese
Protestants of several cities have set Catholics an example by
securing pledges from their people."[1] Another writes, somewhat
wryly, "Many non-Catholic groups have been provided with pledges by
the Chancery office and seem to be very much interested in the
movement. So much so, that one might say that they, in some cases,
take the attitude that they started the offensive."[2] In the
Savannah diocese, "The number of pledges amounted to several thousand
in excess of the total Catholic population of Georgia, because of the
requests from non-Catholics for copies."[3] In Denver, "The Council of
Jewish Women and the Sisterhood of Temple Emmanuel secured 1,000
pledges for their members."[4] In Nashville, "Protestant ministers
supported the movement. Approximately 23,000 pledge cards were supplied
them for distribution in their churches."[5] The Hays office observer
reported 60,000 pledges signed in the Protestant city of Houston, Texas,

---

1. "Report," p. 46.
2. Ibid., p. 240.
3. Ibid., p. 370.
4. Ibid., p. 349.
5. Ibid., p. 362.

where the Protestant Ministerial Alliance "stole the show" from the
Catholics.[1] The New York Times, between June and November of the
campaign year gave forty reports on Protestant activity, mentioning
twenty-seven different groups or leaders of groups. An incomplete
list compiled from the Times, America and the diocesan reports to the
Episcopal Committee, contains the names of fifty-four organizations of
Protestant or Jewish churches, ministers and rabbis who cooperated in
securing pledges, or publicly announced their supplort of the Legion
campaign. The organizations range from local ministerial groups,
through city, state, and regional councils or federations of churches,
to the Federal Council of the Churches of Christ in America.

It is altogether impossible to give a numerical estimate of the
effect of this activity upon the enrollment of members in the Legion
of Decency. Dr. Tippy, as head of the Department of Church and
Social Service of the Federal Council of the Churches of Christ in
America, announced at one stage of the campaign that Protestants
were signing pledges sent out by his organization "by hundreds of
thousands."[2] Christian Century, a national, non-denominational
Protestant weekly, described the Protestant cooperation thus:

> It has been heartening to see the Protestant
> reaction to the launching of this Catholic
> crusade. Seldom has there been as clear an
> illustration of the essential unity of purpose
> of the religious bodies in the realm of social
> and moral action....Thousands of Protestant
> ministers and laity...say: "Thank God that the
> Catholics are at last opening up on this foul
> thing as it deserves! What can we do to help?"[3]

1. Cf. Photoplay, September, 1937, p. 44.
2. The New York times, July 26, 1934.
3. Christian century, LI (June 20, 1934), 822 f.

There seems to be no reason to doubt the statement that Protestants signed by the hundreds of thousands. Whatever the exact number, they represented a substantial contribution to the pressure exerted by the Legion of Decency.

Functional relation of non-Catholic to Catholic members.--At first glance it would seem that the function of the non-Catholic followers was the same as that of the Catholics: to exert pressure upon the film industry by staying away from objectionable pictures. But, as will be seen, social pressure is exerted only to the extent that it is apprehended by those against whom it is directed. There is no reason to suppose that the non-Catholics did not actually stay away from objectionable films. Janes' study indicated that this was the case in Chicago.[1] To the extent that actual box-office shrinkage exerted pressure on the industry, non-Catholics and Catholics were fulfilling the same function.

But the pressure of the Legion was not only in the actual box-office losses; it was also in the threat of future losses. In the exercise of pressure through this threat of future sanction, it seems doubtful that the non-Catholics were fulfilling the same function as the Catholics. Janes quotes a "well-informed Protestant professor" as saying, "the protests of the Protestant denominations in conjunction with the Legion campaign were not taken very seriously by the industry because it knew that these protests could not be backed by actual pressure."[2] Protestant groups had campaigned against

---

1. Robert W. Janes, The Legion of Decency and the motion picture industry, Unpublished M. A. dissertation, University of Chicago, 1939, pp. 3 ff.
2. Ibid., p. 50.

the movies before, with no permanent success. In the industry's
definition of the situation, they did not represent a real threat. But
the Catholics were such a threat. It was to the Catholic Episcopal
Committee that the industry went with its proposals for amendment. It
is immaterial whether or not the industry's was an accurate definition
of the situation; the pressure, if it were to exist at all, had to be
introcepted by the industry.

On the positive side of the ledger, the non-Catholic followers
and their leaders encouraged the Catholic leaders and followers of
the Legion to be vigorous and unyielding in the pursuit of their
objectives, by demonstrating to this minority group that many others
shared their aims. Furthermore, the non-Catholic support made it
impossible for the industry to defy the Catholic demands, or to turn
them aside with the expectation that the non-Catholic majority would
refuse to support the Catholic minority.

Structurally, the non-Catholic followers are to be included with
the Catholic. Functionally, they form part of the actual pressure
group. In military figure, their relation to the Catholic followers
was that of the division which protects the flanks, and raises the
morale of the main attacking force.

Permanent Organization of the Legion

After the motion picture industry's offer to reorganize the
Production Code Administration was put into effect in July, 1934, the
Episcopal Committee began to consider the possibility of keeping the
Legion of Decency in permanent existence. Archbishop McNicholas wrote,

in August,

> Even if the Legion of Decency accomplish its
> immediate purpose of purifying the screen, it
> would seem to have the further permanent purpose
> of keeping the people informed, thereby maintaining
> a healthy public opinion which may prove to the
> producers the wisdom of not returning to their old
> ways of capitalizing on the sins and weaknesses of
> men.[1]

Two months later, Bishop Boyle of the Episcopal Committee, wrote,
"there must be a permanent and a disciplined group to keep watch
on the talking pictures and to act summarily when breaches of decency
occur."[2]

The Bishops, in the General Session of their annual meeting that
November, issued a statement which said, "The Legion of Decency will
be maintained as a permanent protest against everything in the moving
pictures which is subversive of morality."[3]

An Additional Function

The most important structural development found in the permanent
organization of the Legion is the additional function of reviewing
and rating the moral qualities of films.

It seems inevitable that if people were to implement their
pledges to avoid objectionable films, they would have to know in
advance which pictures came within that category.

Yet there were difficulties which postponed the inclusion of a
reviewing group in the Legion organization until the formative period

---

1. "The Episcopal Committee and the problem of evil motion pictures,"
   Ecclesiastical review, XCI (1934), 118.
2. "The Legion of Decency a permanent campaign," ibid., 367 f.
3. "Report," p. 378.

was over. First, there was the practical psychological doubt: would

the blacklisting of a picture give it profitable publicity? Second,

there was a more subtle difficulty for Catholics accustomed to

accepting moral guidance only from authorized religious authorities:

who would decide which pictures were objectionable from a moral

standpoint? Boards of lay reviewers would have no such authority.

Many Bishops were hesitant about the advisability of lending their

approbation to the findings of such boards.[1] Before the Legion arrived

on the scene, the only Catholic group engaged in reviewing films was

the International Federation of Catholic Alumnae. As laywomen, they

had never undertaken the responsibility of issuing moral condemnations

of pictures; they had published only "white" lists of pictures which

could unquestionably be endorsed.[2]

Both of these difficulties were resolved in the time-honored

method which is best described in the tag phrase, solvitur ambulando.

Lists of "condemned" pictures began to make their appearance early in

the campaign. The first of them seems to have appeared in Detroit.[3]

In May, Father Lord announced that his Sodality publication The

Queen's Work would publish each month the names of five pictures which

"notably violate the Code."[4] Soon the Chicago diocesan group, under

the supervision of Father Dinneen, was publishing for local consumption

more or less complete classifications of all the feature films in

circulation at the time. Father Lord switched to this list. So did

1. McNicholas, op. cit., 117.
2. I am indebted to the Reverend Francis X. Talbot, S.J., for many
   years spiritual adviser to the group, for this explanation of their
   policy.
3. Variety, May 13, 1934.
4. The motion pictures betray America, pp. 46 f.

Detroit. In a short time many diocesan papers were using the Chicago
list. Other diocesan papers published only the International
Federation of Catholic Alumnae's list of endorsed pictures.

It became apparent that the publication of a "black list" was
not defeating the Legion's purpose, as many had feared; and the
question of what authority was to be given to these lists, while it
was not definitely settled, was not causing any great commotion.
When the Bishops met in November, they gave their recommendation to
the Chicago list, but left it in the "informal," "unofficial,"
category.[1] The Chicago group, after a year and a half of operation,
ceased to publish their list. In the meantime the I.F.C.A. group in
New York had added to their list of endorsed pictures a classification
of objectionable films; they also stopped publishing aesthetic
appreciations of the pictures. When the Chicago group left the field,
the I.F.C.A. group became the "official" reviewers, under the direction
of a permanent executive secretary from the Archdiocese of New York,
responsible to the Episcopal Committee.

In this way, from a doubtful and unofficial beginning, the
reviewing and listing function developed into an established procedure
structurally integrated into the permanent organization of the Legion.

I.F.C.A. reviewers.--Each year hundreds of feature films are reviewed
and classified by an unpaid, volunteer group of ladies who are
graduates of Catholic colleges and convent schools. A decade before
they took up the Legion work, under the leadership of Mrs. Thomas A.
McGoldrick, they had begun to preview moving pictures, taking advantage

1. "Report," p. 381.

of the Hays office "Open Door" policy. Mrs. McGoldrick continued to direct the group for some years, until poor health interfered; when the Legion of Decency was inaugurated, Mrs. James F. Looram was in charge. Mrs. Looram has been head of the group ever since.

All during the Legion campaign in 1934, the I.F.C.A. group continued to publish their weekly list of endorsed pictures. In January, 1935, they assumed the task of preparing a weekly list for the New York Archdiocesan Council of the Legion of Decency; this list included objectionable, as well as endorsed films. When the New York list became the sole and official list of the National Legion of Decency, a year later, they continued their activity, without sacrificing their identity as an independent organization which carried on many other activities besides the classification of motion pictures.

The number of reviewers in the group fluctuates between sixty and one hundred. In recent years a smaller group from the same organization has functioned on the West Coast; this is a subsidiary group. There is a nucleus of "veteran" reviewers, who have been doing the work since pre-Legion days; this inner group is augmented by some others who have become steady reviewers in more recent years. There is also a group of new recruits, drawn from the ranks of I.F.C.A. members. A "veteran" reviewer has told the author that in the usual course of events reviewers took up the work shortly after graduation from college; continued until marriage and the care of children made it impossible; returned when the children had grown sufficiently to permit activity outside the home. In June, 1942, just about one half of the reviewers were married; the secretary in charge of sending notices to the reviewers estimated that the unmarried reviewers were all under thirty-five years of age. It would seem that somewhat more than one-half of the reviewing staff is composed of permanent members, the others being recruits in the process of training.

Recruits must pass through a six months period of training and indoctrination. During this time they attend weekly previews held for their exclusive attendance at the M-G-M preview room. The author attended two such sessions in June, 1942. At each there were about twenty young ladies. Mrs. Thomas Bannin, who had formerly edited the I.F.C.A.'s weekly "Endorsed Motion Pictures," was the regular leader of these sessions. In Mrs. Bannin's absence, Mary Sheridan, film critic, led one of the sessions. The pictures were viewed with no preliminaries, but at the end of the showing, individual opinions were solicited, reasons for the different ratings given by the Legion were explained, and applications made to particular points raised by the film they had seen.

In addition to these training sessions, every month the Motion Picture Department of the I.F.C.A. has a meeting at its headquarters; here there is discussion of pictures which have provoked differences of opinion, or have offered some special difficulty. At one of these meetings, attended by the author in April, 1944, there were twenty-five "veteran" reviewers present. Only the novice group discusses a film immediately after the showing; the regular reviewers make their reports privately and separately. Consequently many reviewers have questions to be discussed at the monthly meetings.

Assignments to reviewers are sent out from the midtown office of the I.F.C.A. in New York. Reports are sent back to this office. Thence they are telephoned or mailed to the Legion of Decency office

which is thirteen blocks further uptown. At the Legion of Decency office,
Mrs. Looram, head of the Motion Picture Department of the I.F.C.A.,
receives the reports and presents them to Monsignor McClafferty,
Executive Secretary of the Legion of Decency. Mrs. Looram is the
organizational link between the I.F.C.A. and the Legion of Decency.

Consultors.--Pictures which have been condemned by the I.F.C.A.
reviewers, or have raised serious questions among them, are submitted
to the Consultors' Committee of the Legion of Decency. The Committee
of Consultors is made up of sixteen Catholic clergymen and thirteen
Catholic laymen. Not all of the clergy are consulted on each case;
the sixteen priests form a panel from which an average of three or four
are drawn for each occasion. An effort is made, however, to have all
the laymen view each disputed picture. Their number includes a labor
leader, a dean of a law school, an administrator in a school of social
service and two lawyers. They were selected as representative of a
cross-section of society, rather than for any influence or prestige they
might possess in the sub-groups from which they come.

Executive Secretary.--The final decision as to the rating of
pictures, and all matters of ordinary policy are in the hands of the
Very Reverend John J. McClafferty, Executive Secretary to the
Episcopal Committee on Motion Pictures since December, 1936.
Monsignor McClafferty is assisted by the Reverend Patrick J.
Masterson[1] and the Reverend Brendan Larnen, O.P. The executive
secretary and his assistants are the organizational link between the

---

1. Father Masterson is at present serving as chaplain to the armed
   forces.

reviewing activities and the Episcopal Committee.

Structure of the Legion After Ten Years

Most of the functions of the Legion of Decency now radiate from
the reviewing and listing activity. A skeletonal outline of the
present-day structure of the Legion will make this clear.

Episcopal Committee.--The Episcopal Committee maintains direction
of major policy. In addition, through the executive secretary, it
directs the activities of the reviewers.

The local Bishops.--Local Bishops now have a triple function.
The first is the maintenance of membership, which is accomplished
through this device: each year they have the Legion pledge renewed
in all the parishes of their dioceses at all the Masses on the
Sunday after December 8, which is the Feast of the Immaculate
Conception, patronal Feast of the United States.

The second is the organization of protests against the showing
of films which have been condemned by the Legion. Some Bishops do
more than others in this regard; some, apparently, do nothing.

The third is the important function of providing contact between
the members of the Legion and the Legion ratings. This is accomplished chiefly through the publication of these lists in the diocesan
press. Most diocesan papers carry the list. Supplementary to this, in
some dioceses, is the posting of the list in the vestibules of
churches, on the bulletin boards of the parochial schools. Some
dioceses have organized Councils of the Legion of Decency to carry on
educational and publicity work. The structure of these diocesan
groups varies in different dioceses; the two most usual procedures are

to build them upon existing parochial units, or upon the trans-
parochial diocesan Councils of Catholic Men and Catholic Women.

The followers.--Two types of members may now be distinguished.
First, there are those who are ready to refuse their patronage to
any picture condemned by the Legion reviewers. Their membership is
"latent," as Coyle[1] puts it; that is, they are inactive "unless called
into action by some emergency," such as a Class C rating given to a
major film.

Second, there are those who refuse to patronize pictures which
the Legion declares to be objectionable in part. This class of members
consults the Legion's ratings regularly; there is thus a certain
amount of constant activity.

In different ways, the two classes of members are exercising real
pressure on the film industry. In the case of the latent members, the
pressure is potential, ready to be activated when a major film is
condemned. All who renew the pledge annually must be presumed to be
in this class. In the case of the second class of members, the
pressure is actual, a reduction in the box office receipts of the
pictures rated objectionable in part. There is no way of counting
these members. That there are some, enough to make their absence felt
from certain types of pictures, at least, is indicated by the fact
that the industry makes occasional efforts to have pictures raised
above the objectionable classification. It is the policy of the
Episcopal Committee to have this number increased.

----

1. Coyle, op. cit., p. 96.

CHAPTER III

THE ENDS OF THE LEGION OF DECENCY

Introduction

There are two distinct series of questions raised when one asks "why?" the Legion of Decency operates.

The first series is related to the subjective state of mind of the Legion agents. One may ask if the leaders of the Legion have "real" aims which differ from their ostensible aims. Pursuing this line of inquiry such questions as the following would be posed. What economic advantages accrue to the Legion leaders? Are they seeking political power, or authoritative, dominating control over the motion picture industry? Are their activities determined by imperative demands for inner, psychological satisfactions? Is there some wish, drive, sentiment, some frustration, some transcendent sex urge "behind" or "underneath" their observable course of action and statements of aims?[1]

These are interesting questions. It is perhaps possible that some of them can be given objective answers by the methods of empirical science. But the author has been able neither to collect the life histories of the principal agents nor to subject the individuals to the control experiments which would be necessary to test the validity of any hypotheses he might erect on such premisses. Regretfully, therefore, this aspect of the Legion of Decency must be excluded from the scope of this work.

---

1. Cf. Hadley Cantril, The psychology of social movements, New York, John Wiley and Sons, 1941, pp. 30-52; also J. Stewart Burgess, "The study of modern social movements as a means for clarifying the process of social action," Social forces, XXII (1944), 271 f.

The second series of questions is related to the objective situation created by the Legion's activities. These are more prosaic questions; but there is data to answer them, and inferences drawn from that data are subject to check and control by testing the validity of the reasoning processes used in arriving at them.

The end of any social action, in this objective sense, is the "future state of affairs toward which the process of action is oriented."[1] More precisely, it is that aspect of the future state of affairs which is different from what would have been had the action not taken place.

The changes in the motion picture situation which would not have occurred if the Legion of Decency had not been in operation are the ends of the Legion activity. Conspicuous among these is the reorganization and maintenance of the Production Code Administration's machinery for enforcing the provisions of the Code. This, as will be seen in the next chapter, was an intermediate end, a means to a further end. Industry self-regulation was chosen from among several alternative means simply because it seemed most likely to result in the production of "only such motion pictures as may conform with reasonable moral standards."[2] Insofar as moral standards are the expression of values,[3] the ends of the Legion may be equated with the values actively supported by the Legion.

---

1. Parsons, Structure of social action, p. 44.
2. Statement of Episcopal Committee, Cincinnati, June, 1934, "Report," p. 27.
3. By "value" is understood: "The substantive quality of any object, no matter what its ontological status, which gives rise to a mental and neural state of readiness exerting a directive or dynamic influence upon the response to such object." This definition is compounded from propositions in Ralph Barton Perry, General theory of value, New York, Longmans, Green and Co., 1926, p. 116, and in Gordon W. Allport, "Attitudes," A handbook of social psychology (ed. Carl Murchison), Worcester, Clark University Press, 1935, p. 810.

A word of precaution is needed here. The values of the Legion
are usually expressed in a negative way. Underlying these negative
expressions may be whole complexes of positive values. Thus, when the
Legion objects, as it does so often, to "light treatment of marriage"
in a film, the positive values implicit in the objection may be many.
There may be concern for marriage as a sacrament, as an institution
which safeguards the procreation and education of children, as a noble
relationship of love between husband and wife, etc., etc. Analysis of
this sort can be continued indefinitely; but without data to check and
control it, it is worthless. Unfortunately, there is little evidence
upon which to base this type of analysis. This chapter, accordingly,
will be restricted to pointing out the main fields of human
co-existence in which the Legion considered that the movies were
threatening its values.

Values, Folsom and Strelsky note, are best discovered "by
observing the content of communication."[1] The communications which
reveal the Legion's values fall into two categories. There are,
first, generic statements which are found in the rules of the
Production Code, in the pronouncements of Bishops during the Legion
campaign, and in the explanatory treatises which guide the judgments
of the reviewers. There are, secondly, the recorded expressions of
the reviewers' value judgments, which are summarily stated in the
published reasons for Legion objection to films, and are more completely
stated in the ballots of the individual reviewers.

These categories will be studied in turn, the whole study being

1. Joseph K. Folsom and Nikander Strelsky, "Russian values and character--
   a preliminary exploration," American sociological review, IX (1944)
   296 f.

prefaced by a general consideration of the Legion's attitude towards
entertainment as such.

Entertainment as a Value

Entertainment as such is not a negative value to the Legion of
Decency. The end of the Legion is not, therefore, the elimination of
entertainment from the motion picture.

The Catholic religion does not proscribe entertainment. Saint
Thomas Aquinas says that entertainment is a right of human nature, which
is so constituted that it needs diversion and recreation.[1]

What is commonly called the puritanical attitude toward amusement,
which found an echo in Bossuet's dictum that one "ne s'amuse pas quand
on est chretien," derives from the theory that human nature is
essentially corrupt. Gillet points out that this is not Catholic
doctrine:

> Il a tort de croire qu'il ne peut y en avoir de bons,
> a cause d'une pretendue corruption de la nature
> humaine.... Au contraire, saint Thomas, avec le
> Concile de Trente, rejette nettement l'idee d'une
> corruption originelle et hereditaire de la nature
> humaine.[2]

True, the early Fathers directed invectives against the conditions
of the theater of their day. And later legislation of the Church
condemned outrageous performances in churches and cemeteries. But
there has been never a "final stand taken against theatrical matters
or the theatre."[3]

---

1. Summa theologica, 1-2, q. 178, a. 2.
2. M. S. Gillet, "Theatre," Dictionnaire apologetique de la foi catholique, Paris, Gabriel Beauchesne, 1928, t. iv, 1634.
3. Matthew A. Coyle, C.S.C., "The Church and the theatre," Ecclesiastical
   review, XCIII (1935), 138.

If the Church has looked upon the theater and the motion picture
with something less than benignant approval, it is, says Girerd,
because "elle les juge dangereux, ce qu'ils sont en effet, non qu'elle
les proclame immoreaux."[1]

That the contemporary Church has preserved the attitude of Saint
Thomas toward entertainment is revealed in the words of Pius XI:
"Recreation in its manifold variety has become a necessity of people
who labor under the fatiguing conditions of modern industry."[2]

The formulators of the Production Code expressed the same attitude:
"Mankind has always recognized the importance of entertainment and its
value in rebuilding the bodies and souls of human beings."

During the Legion campaign, Catholic Bishops reiterated similar
expressions almost every time they made public statements. An official
statement of the Episcopal Committee said: "The Committee is not hostile
to the entertainment business. In fact it recognizes entertainment as
a virtual necessity in modern life."[3] The Bishops wanted to reassure
their followers that their leaders were not fanatics; they wanted the
industry to know that they did not wish to drive it out of business.

As a final confirmation of the point, the Legion's reviewing
staff registers no objection to western "horse operas," musical
comedies, and other pictures which claim no other function than that of
diversion.

---

1. Francois Girerd, "Theatre et cinema--I. Morale," Dictionnaire
   pratique des connaissances religieuses, Paris, Libraire Letouzey et
   Ane, 1928, t. xvi, 617.
2. On motion pictures, p. 7.
3. "Report," p. 26.

Generic Expressions of Values

The Production Code

Values implicit in the Code.--The Production Code has three
sections. The first consists of a preamble, a brief statement of
general principles, and a catalog of particular applications. The
second is a lengthy statement of "reasons supporting" the first section.
The third is in the form of a resolution setting forth machinery for
uniform interpretation of the preceding. This last is not of concern in
the present context.

The preamble, in the first section, and its supporting reasons, in
the second section, are concerned with the responsibility to society
which is assumed by the producers of motion picture art and entertainment.

The general principles, and their supporting reasons, elaborate
the proposition that "no picture shall be produced which will lower the
moral standards of those who see it."

The particular applications lay down norms to be followed in the
treatment of certain subjects; the supporting reasons explain how
violation of these norms is apt to lower the moral standards of the
members of the audience.

The particular applications are grouped under twelve headings:
(1) crimes against the law, (2) sex, (3) vulgarity, (4) obscenity,
(5) dances, (6) profanity, (7) costume, (8) religion, (9) locations,
(10) national feelings, (11) titles, (12) repellent subjects.

Analysis of the particular applications shows that they are all
concerned with behavior relating to one of the following: the individual human being, relations between the sexes, property, law and
religion.

The positive values revealed in these standards are: (1) the inviolability of the human person, both (a) physically, inasmuch as murder, revenge and brutality are proscribed, and (b) mentally, inasmuch as it is forbidden to present "low, disgusting, unpleasant subjects," "repellent subjects," and such as give offense to "national feelings": (2) the institution of private property, inasmuch as its possession is not to be molested by theft and destruction; (3) the institution of monogamous marriage and chastity; (4) the sacredness of law; and (5) the sacredness of religion.

In the reasons supporting these applications, it is stated that standards embodying these values may be endangered by the movies in one of several ways. First, favorable attitudes towards the standards and their values are apt to be broken down by the presentation of non-conforming behavior as proper and attractive. Second, favorable attitudes are apt to be weakened by the repeated portrayal of such violations as murder and brutality, which tend to harden the audience to the thought and fact of their commission. Third, films may facilitate violations of the accepted standards by detailing methods of crime. Fourth, pictures may directly incite to behavior which violates the standards by portrayals which stimulate responses of the "lower and baser element" of the sexual emotions.

The Production Code and other codes.--There had been several attempts to set up standards by which to judge the morality of motion pictures previous to the Production Code. The more important ones include: the eight rules of the National Board of Censorship of Motion

Pictures, formulated before 1913;[1] the twenty-four rules of the
Pennsylvania State Board of Censors, in 1918;[2] the thirteen resolutions of the National Association of the Motion Picture Industry,
in 1921;[3] and the eleven "Don'ts" and twenty-five "Be Carefuls" of
the Hays office in 1927.[4]

Except for the fact that the "Don'ts" and "Be Carefuls" were
incorporated into the "Particular Applications" of the Production
Code, there is no discernible genetic relation between the Code and
any of the previous formulae. Yet there are important similarities.

The table on the next page shows that the fields of behavior
selected for mention in the Code differ from those listed in other sets
of standards only in minor respects.

In the Code, but not in any other list, are rules relating to
revenge, and to the use of liquor in American life.

Not specifically mentioned in the Code, but found in the standards
of the Pennsylvania censors, and of the N.A.M.P.I. resolutions, are
provisions regarding gambling and drunkenness. It may be noted, in
this connection, that in surveys conducted by the General Federation
of Women's Clubs, the Minneapolis Women's Cooperative Alliance, and
the Lancaster (Pennsylvania) Ministerial Alliance, drinking and
gambling scenes had met with disapproval.[5]

The comparison shows that the Code differs very little from the
other sets of standards in the values it seeks to preserve. There are

1. Exhibitors of motion pictures and the National Board of Censorship,
   New York, n.d., pp. 4 f.
2. Quoted in Donald R. Young, Motion pictures, a study in social legislation, Ph.D. dissertation, University of Pennsylvania, 1922, Appendix.
3. Ibid., pp. 13 f.
4. Op. cit.
5. Young, op. cit., pp. 22 ff.

TABLE 2

SUBJECTS LISTED IN THE PRODUCTION CODE AND THEIR
PRESENCE OR ABSENCE IN OTHER SELECTED CODES[1]

Subjects	National Board of Censorship of Motion Pictures	Pennsylvania State Board of Censorship	National Association Motion Picture Industry	"Don'ts" and "Be Carefuls"	Production Code
Person					
Physical					
Murder	O	x	O	x	x
Brutality	x	x	x	x	x
Revenge	O	O	O	O	x
Mental					
"Vulgarity"	x	x	x	x	x
Offense to national feelings	O	x	O	x	x
Property					
Crime	x	x	x	x	x
Methods of crime	x	x	x	x	x
Sex					
Illicit relations	"Obscenity in all its forms."	x	x	x	x
Scenes of passion		x	x	x	x
Exposure of body		x	x	x	x
"Obscene" dances		x	x	O	x
White slavery		x	x	x	x
Childbirth scenes		x	O	x	x
Sex hygiene		x	O	x	x
Sex perversion		O	O	x	x
Miscegenation		O	O	x	x
Children's sex organs		O	O	x	x
Law					
Ridicule of law	O	O	x	x	x
Illegal drug traffic	O	x	x	x	x
Liquor in U. S. life	O	O	O	O	x
Religion					
Offense to beliefs	x	x	x	x	x

1. x denotes presence of similar provision; O denotes absence of similar provision.

Sources: The Production Code and other sets of standards as cited in the text.

other important differences between the Code and the previous instruments;
these will be treated in the next chapter.

Statements of the Bishops in the Campaign

When the Episcopal Committee gave its blessing to the film
industry's offer to tighten the machinery for enforcement of the Code,
it implied that the values the Legion wished to support were to some
extent identical with those embodied in the provisions of the Code.

We would expect, then, that in the recruiting campaign the local
Bishops would have expressed their concern for the preservation of
values corresponding to those stressed in the Production Code. But the
Bishops could not suppose that their potential followers were familiar
with the details of the Code. They had to appeal for direct support of
the standards and values which were threatened. This fact calls for an
examination of the Bishops' utterances, to see which values they were
most concerned about. Then we can compare them with the Code. Finally,
we may ask whether or not these were the same values the followers of the
Legion were concerned about.

Values of concern to the Bishops.--The Episcopal Committee's
"Report" contains sixty-eight communications from the Bishops,
consisting of articles, addresses, and letters to the clergy and the
laity of their respective dioceses.[1] Analysis of these communications
shows that the Bishops' charges against the films were: (1) that pictures
were such as to lower the moral standards of their audiences; (2) that
they offended chiefly in the spheres of sex, crime, "good taste" and

---

1. "Report," pp. 5-205.

religion; and (3) that they were especially dangerous for the young.

It is impossible to make very accurate quantitative statements about the relative frequency of the respective charges. But in order to indicate in a general way the relative emphasis placed by the Bishops, the author has enumerated the frequency with which the various charges are found in the documents. In this enumeration, words and phrases repeated by a Bishop are counted only once in each communication. But many of the expressions are used synonymously, e.g., "immoral" and "menace to morals," "filthy" and "salacious," etc. These are counted separately. Despite these limitations, the general trend of the emphasis appears in the figures.

There were two hundred and four general characterizations of the films as tending to lower moral standards.

The particular spheres mentioned were: (1) sex, one hundred and ninety-six times; complaints were evenly divided between the movies' approval of violation of the sex standards and their stimulation of sex responses in the members of the audiences; (2) crime, fifty-three times, usually without distinguishing crimes against the person from crimes against property; (3) offenses against "good taste," twenty times. Thirty-six references to the harmful effects of movies upon youth were counted.

Comparison with Code.--In general, the values over which the Bishops expressed concern were similar to those embodied in the Code. The category "law," found in the Code, but not in the Bishops' statements, is implicit in their generalized denunciation of "crime." Many of the specific provisions in the Code under the heading "sex" were not mentioned at all by the Bishops. One of these, viz., "miscegenation," is not in conflict with the moral standards of the Church. The use of liquor is not in itself an offense against the standards of the Catholic religion. Omission of the others could be attributed either to the fact that the Bishops did not consider that the films were offending in those respects, or to the fact that they did not consider offenses along these lines to be serious threats to the standards and values they were upholding. Apart from these minor variations, the Bishops' statements follow the general line of the Code's values, with the greatest emphasis upon those concerned with sex.

Values of the Bishops and those of the followers.--It might be fair to say that since the Bishops initiated the Legion movement and set its ends, the values stressed by the Bishops were also values for the bulk of the members who followed their leadership.

Yet it could be questioned whether these values were recognized by the followers with direct or with indirect recognition.[1] That is, were these values personally introcepted[2] by the followers, or did they merely accept their leaders' dictum that they were worth preserving?

There is no direct answer to that question. No polls were taken; there is no literature of communications from the followers. There is

1. Cf. Timasheff, Sociology of law, p. 89.
2. Gordon W. Allport, Personality, New York, Henry Holt and Company, 1937, p. 217, n. 1, "The term introception, originated by W. Stern, stands for the adoption by an individual of cultural standards (conventions, morals, ideals) into his own personal system of motives and desires, or the incorporation of the interests and values of other human beings into his own life."

twofold evidence, however, pointing toward direct recognition on the part of the followers.

The first is negative evidence. It consists in the fact that the text of the pledge which was circulated, and the content of the communications from the Bishops to their followers, lay no stress on the "follow the leader" incentive. Their general tone is not, "We, your leaders, know best." Rather, the short-comings of the movies are directly set forth with the unstated assumption that such violations strike at values which are highly esteemed by the followers.

The second evidence comes from Lupton A. Wilkinson, whom the Hays office sent on a tour during the Legion campaign, covering eighty-two cities and towns in the United States. His principal task was to ascertain the effect of the Legion campaign in each locality. Secondarily, he was to try to find out "what the average American man and woman wanted in their movies--and what they didn't want."[1]

While Wilkinson's chief sources of information were newspaper and motion picture men, they were at that time in a relatively good position to be acquainted with the attitudes of the "average man." Wilkinson's daily reports to the home office showed that he was a good reporter, very objective.

Wilkinson summed up the main objections to the movies thus:

1. Injected vulgarities.
2. Plots of young people who play fast and loose with life and come out winners. Ditto about married women.
3. Triangle plots where the two cheaters win.
4. All screen treatment or suggestion of abnormal sex relations.[2]

---

1. Photoplay, September, 1937, p. 44.
2. Ibid.

When it is noted that in his explanation what he means by "injected vulgarities," Wilkinson speaks of "a labored sex-crack or hot scene," it can be seen that his report shows broad agreement with the Bishops. His first item is concerned with the films' stimulation of sex responses in the audience. His second and third are concerned with approval given in the films to violations of the sex standards. These were the two main elements of the Bishops' attack on the movies. His fourth item was not a main concern of the Bishops; on the other hand he does not mention at all the offenses in the sphere of crime and religion. These latter were, however, relatively slight concerns of the Bishops. Finally, their emphasis upon the harmful effects of movies on the young is reflected in Wilkinson's comment on his second item:

> The stories were bad art and bad life--things are not that easy. Fathers didn't want their daughters exposed to such philosophy. Husbands, especially of young wives, didn't want Honeybunch's head filled with such phony life tips.[1]

Judicial Norms for Reviewers

For some years before the Legion of Decency, the Motion Picture Bureau of the International Federation of Catholic Alumnae had been issuing each week a four page list of current "Endorsed Motion Pictures." This list contained the names of films which they considered "suitable for church halls, Catholic schools, or family night programs," or "suitable for mature audiences but inappropriate for church halls and school showings." Pictures within both categories were rated esthetically as "good," or "very good." Objectionable

---

1. Photoplay, September 1937, p. 44.
2. Ibid.

pictures were not mentioned.

When the I.F.C.A. accepted the task of listing pictures for the Legion they shifted their focus, to a certain extent, from the praiseworthy to the blameworthy. This was in the nature of their new function, that of implementing the Legion pledge by pointing out the pictures to be avoided. Instead of dismissing objectionable pictures without comment, now they had to carefully distinguish them according to the kind and degree of their offensiveness, and they had to state clearly the reasons for their objections.

To acquire the necessary set of judicial norms for carrying out this task, I.F.C.A. reviewers study Martin Quigley's Decency in Motion Pictures,[1] the Production Code, and two treatises: How to Judge the Morality of Motion Pictures,[2] and The Morals of the Screen.[3]

Quigley's book provides the reviewers with the historical background of the conflict which led to their activity, and it includes the text of the Production Code. The Code gives the reviewers a statement of what to expect from films.

How to Judge the Morality of Motion Pictures.--This brochure describes itself as "A popular guide to right standards in motion picture entertainment, authorized by the Episcopal Committee on Motion Pictures for the Legion of Decency." Its eight pages summarily set forth the moral significance and influence of the movies, the purpose of the Legion of Decency, the nature of the Production Code, the Legion's attitude towards what should and what should not be portrayed in the

1. Quigley, op. cit.,
2. How to judge the morality of motion pictures, Washington, D.C., National Catholic Welfare Conference, n.d.
3. Richard Dana Skinner, "The morals of the screen," Washington, D.C., National Catholic Welfare Conference, reprinted from The Catholic educational review, October, 1935.

movies, and six condensed examples of the objectionable types of pictures.

The general thesis of the pamphlet is that the Legion, while it condemns obscenities, salaciousness, suggestiveness, is principally concerned with films "which present false moral standards which, in turn, lower traditional morality."

> The Legion of Decency is concerned not so much about the materials selected for a story as about the moral treatment of those materials.... Does the story preach an immoral doctrine? Does it propose a false estimate of human conduct? These are the all-important questions.[1]

"Traditional morality" is explained to mean:

> Such principles of conduct as the following: "Murder is wrong. Stealing is wrong. Perjury is wrong. Honor is due to father and mother." These standards, together with many relating to sex, follow from the code of right and wrong written into the consciences of men by God Himself. They have been generally known and accepted during all the centuries, not only by Christians, but by Jews, pagans and by men of no religious affiliation. They are expressed in the Ten Commandments.[2]

Five of the six examples given in the pamphlet offer generalized illustrations of the way in which the movies "preach" immoral doctrines. "Many films," it is asserted, "by their insidious and attractive presentation of false standards, induce their patrons to change their lifelong convictions and to believe that, occasionally, at least, certain sins are virtues and certain virtues are sins."[3] The first of these examples

---

1. How to judge the morality of motion pictures, p. 8.
2. Ibid., pp. 4 f.
3. Ibid., p. 7.

is quoted here in full:

> "Picture 'A'".--This is a deeply moving triangle story.
> It is entirely devoid of salacious details, but it
> proposes the doctrine that when a man's wife is selfish
> and unsympathetic he is entirely justified in turning to
> another woman for love and happiness. In short, the film
> condones and justifies adultery. It does this, not by
> ethical arguments but by emotional appeal. Deeply
> stirred by the picture, many of those witnessing it are
> apt to sympathize with the hero, approve his conduct, and
> thus change their former convictions. They may be led to
> believe that under certain circumstances adultery is
> excusable. Here is a false moral standard, wholly at
> variance with traditional beliefs.[1]

The generic charge of "immorality" made by the Bishops during the

Legion campaign has been defined in this pamphlet to include any

violation of the traditional code of the Ten Commandments. The

specific values of monogamy, chastity, the inviolability of the human

person, etc., are presented without any apparent change of emphasis.

But there is relatively less stress laid upon the stimulation of sex

responses in the audience. The great emphasis is upon the emotionally

alluring presentation of behavior at variance with the accepted

standards, especially in the sphere of sex relations.

The Morals of the Screen.--This treatise offers a more detailed,

technical exposition of the ways in which films may threaten the

accepted values and standards. It is not concerned with explaining

which values and standards are acceptable.

Its author was a veteran dramatic critic. He distinguishes the

theme, the plot and the treatment of the film story. Violations of

the standards may occur in any one or any combination of these.

The theme can be summarized in the form of a question and an

---

1. How to judge the morality of motion pictures, p. 5.

answer. "The question is usually the problem put up to the main character in the play and the answer is the way the main character solves that problem."[1] It is the theme which "largely determines the moral value of a play."[2] The theme is immoral if the answer to the problem involves a course of action which is opposed to the accepted standards and is at the same time presented as proper and approved.

The plot is that which "gives to a theme its particular circumstances of time, place and character."[3] The same theme may be found in the plots of classical antiquity, of Shakespeare and of the stories of modern gangsters. The treatment embraces such matters as "the author's detailed stage directions and dialogue."[4]

Both the plot and the treatment may offend in two ways. The first is by depicting with approval or allure characters or behavior which run counter to "current standards of good taste and convention."[5] The second is by presenting thoughts, words or actions which "arouse a state of mind which, nine times out of ten, leads to immoral actions."[6] This latter "relates closely to the old established Catholic view of the 'occasions of sin.'"[7]

In this latter category Skinner puts gangster films and "suggestive" pictures. The theme of gangster movies is usually beyond

---

1. Skinner, op. cit., p. 1.
2. Ibid., p. 2.
3. Ibid., p. 3.
4. Ibid.
5. Ibid., p. 4.
6. Ibid.
7. Ibid.

reproach, but their plots are excessively concerned with crime, or
their treatment glorifies crime, or it displays murder and violence
with excessive realism, becoming "an incentive to criminal emotions
and reactions."[1] "Suggestive" pictures belong in this category because
their realistic "display of sexual passions" is a "direct occasion of
increased immorality."[2]

Skinner's distinction between theme and treatment has been incorporated into the form of the reports which are filled out by the
reviewers. His emphasis upon thematic violation is in line with the
"Reasons Supporting" the Code provisions, with the Bishops' utterance
during the campaign and with the trend of thought in How to Judge the
Morality of Motion Pictures.

Malcolm Willey has stressed the same point in his discussion of
the influence of modern communications upon the folkways and mores. His
conclusion, after offering an example of a recent movie, is as follows:

> No summary can possibly indicate the deviation
> from accepted values that this film reveals and makes
> acceptable. No summary can suggest the glamor and
> excitement evoked by the picture. As entertainment,
> it is of a high order--but what is its effect? It is
> not intended here to evaluate the picture on any
> ethical grounds, but it is suggested that a romantic
> and alluring presentation of emotionally charged
> values that run counter to the existing mores must
> have its social consequences.[3]

Skinner's norms have been modified in one particular by the Legion
reviewers. Instead of focussing attention on the "main character,"
exclusively, Legion reviewers attend to whatever characters there may

---

1. Skinner, op. cit., p. 5.
2. Ibid.
3. Willey, "Communication agencies and the volume of propaganda," The
   annals, CLXXIX (May, 1935), 199.

be with whom the audience tends to identify itself. They call such a character a "sympathetic character." He must not adopt attitudes or practices which violate the standards, or condone them. This makes it possible for the "main character" to be utterly vicious while the film as a whole is unobjectionable because the sympathetic character or characters react properly. On the other hand there have been objections to films because minor, but sympathetic characters have offended. Such films usually are found in "Unobjectionable in part" listings.

In this connection it should be pointed out that this norm is not identical with that of "Compensating Moral Values" described in Martin's Hollywood's Movie Commandments[1] as one of the norms of the Production Code Administration. According to Martin's description, two of the four compensating moral values are "suffering" and "punishment and retribution."

> Wrong-doing, whether intentional or unintentional, must be shown to bring suffering to the wrong-doer to establish the fact that it is inevitably painful, unpleasant, unprofitable and productive of unhappiness. Where a sin or a wrong is not forsaken, and the wrong-doer is not repentant, the story must indicate that some definite punishment ensues for the unregenerate character.[2]

The Legion's norm is that violations of the standards must not be presented alluringly or with approval. Suffering, punishment or retribution are irrelevant, except insofar as they may serve to counteract the allure or to indicate disapproval. Not every wrong-doer, according to the Legion norm, must suffer or be punished. Nor,

---

1. Olga J. Martin, Hollywood's movie commandments, New York, The H. W. Wilson Company, 1937.
2. Ibid., pp. 99 f.

on the other hand, is suffering or punishment of itself always
sufficient to undo the effect of alluring and approving portrayal of
deviations from the standards.

It may be noted that the original version of the Code, as formulated by Father Lord and Martin Quigley, contains the norm: "Crime
need not always be punished, as long as the audience is made to know
that it is wrong."[1]

Particular Expressions of Values

The best source of information concerning Legion values is, of
course, the judgments it has passed on motion pictures during the
ten years of its existence.

Data for the period ending in February, 1936, during which Chicago
was the chief reviewing center, is fragmentary. For the succeeding
period, however, there are two classes of data. The first is composed
of the published summaries of reasons for objections.[2] Here are all the
reasons for the condemnation of all films on the "C" list, except for
a half dozen of the earlier pictures. Here, too, since 1939, are the
reasons for the objections to all "B" pictures. The second class of
data is composed of the reports filed by Legion reviewers for all the
pictures they have reviewed. Eight to twelve reports are received on
almost every film; more are received for questionable pictures.
During the two years from 1936 to 1938, 26,348 reports were filed.
Inspection of all reports would have been impossible. One hundred and

1. Martin, op. cit., p. 280.
2. The Legion of Decency films reviewed, New York, The Legion of Decency;
   an annual publication since November, 1937. Reasons for those "C"
   pictures which were condemned before 1939 are given in "Class 'C'
   Pictures Previously Reviewed and Reasons for their Classification,"
   mimeographed, n.d.

sixty reports were filed on six major films which were condemned by the Legion in their original versions. These have been studied.

The following study of the Legion's values-in-action, then will be based upon (1) published summary reasons for objection to "C" pictures and certain "B" pictures; (2) unpublished reports on six major condemned pictures.

Published Summary Reasons

Forty-seven "C" pictures.--In the seven and one-half years which ended in November, 1943, the Legion of Decency placed fifty-three pictures on its condemned, or "C" list. This number does not include the films which were condemned at first and then reclassified after the picture had been revised.

With one exception, all of these films were either "quickies" produced and distributed independently in this country for showing in less respectable theaters, or they were foreign-made films which show only in centers with large foreign language speaking populations. The single exception was the Howard Hughes production "The Outlaw," produced in 1943, not as yet given general release. This film was not granted the seal of the Production Code Administration.

For six of these pictures, during the year 1936, reasons for condemnation were not published. For the remaining forty-seven, the published lists give, in summary fashion, one or more reasons for condemnation. Some examples of the way the reasons are published follow:

> Smashing the Vice Racket--John Melville--Objection: Prostitution and white slavery subject material of picture; immodest dress and costume; double-meaning lines; obscene dancing and implications. [1940][1]

---

1. Legion of Decency films reviewed, Nov., 1939-Nov., 1940, p. 30.

Lash of the Penitentes--Stewart Production--Objection: The
film contains many very suggestive, lewd and sadistic scenes.
[1941][1]
Roi, Le (French) (The King)--Film Modernes, Les--Trio Films--
Objection: Crime is presented as attractive; virtue is
ridiculed and adultery is condoned. [1942][2]
Passion Island (La Isla de la Passion) (Mexican)--E.M.A.S.A.
--Maya Film Distributing Corp.--Objection: Immoral in
treatment. Dialogue, costumes and situations are objectionable.
[1943][3]

Of the one hundred and three objections listed for these forty-
seven pictures, seventy-three were concerned with sex. There were
forty-five objections to stimulation of sex responses in the audience
through "suggestive" sequences, dialogue, costuming and dances. Nine
themes were objected to because the approved choice of action involved
illicit sex relations. Nineteen objections concerned plots which dealt
with white slavery, venereal disease, and the "abortions racket." Two
plots were condemned because they dealt with nudist colonies, one
because it dealt with lesbianism and another with "debauchery."

Other reasons for condemnation were: themes which indicated
approval of suicide, murder, dishonesty and crime; plots which were
built around illicit traffic in drugs; treatment which condoned criminal
and anti-religious attitudes, and treatment which created a "sordid
atmosphere" by unrelieved presentation of murder, suicide, and brutality.

One hundred and fifty-seven "B" pictures.--Between November, 1939
and November, 1943, the Legion put two hundred and three pictures in the
objectionable in part, or "B" list. One hundred and fifty-seven of these
were pictures produced by the eight major producers in Hollywood. The

1. Legion of Decency films reviewed, Nov., 1940-Nov., 1941, p. 29.
2. Ibid., Nov., 1941-Nov., 1942, p. 29.
3. Ibid., Nov., 1942-Nov., 1943, p. 28.

others were quickies or foreign films. We shall confine our attention
to the major pictures. Two hundred and fifty-three objections to these
films were listed.

One hundred and ninety-one of the objections were concerned with
sex. One hundred and thirty-one of these--fifty-one percent of all
objection to "B" pictures--referred to "suggestive" sequences, dialogue,
costumes and dances. Almost all of the other objections in this field

TABLE 3

REASONS FOR CONDEMNATION OF FORTY-SEVEN
"C" PICTURES, 1936 TO 1943

	Theme	Plot	Treatment	Total
Person				
Physical				
Murder	3	0	0	3
Suicide	7	0	0	7
Mental				
"Sordid atmosphere"	0	0	6	6
Property				
Crime	1	0	4	5
Dishonesty	2	0	0	2
Sex				
Illicit relations	9	0	0	9
"Suggestive"	0	0	45	45
White slavery	0	7	0	7
Venereal disease	0	5	0	5
"Abortion racket"	0	3	0	3
Nudist camps	0	2	0	2
Lesbianism	0	1	0	1
"Debauchery"	0	1	0	1
Law				
Illicit drug traffic	0	2	0	2
Religion				
Ridicule of	0	0	5	5
Total	22	21	60	103

Sources: Legion of Decency Films Reviewed, Nov., 1939-Nov., 1940; Nov.,
1940-Nov., 1941; Nov., 1941-Nov., 1942; Nov., 1942-Nov., 1943;
for "C" pictures before November, 1939, "Class 'C' Pictures
Previously Reviewed and Reasons for their Classification,"
mimeographed.

concern the institution of marriage. Thirty-two of these were labelled "light treatment of marriage." These objections referred to pictures, mostly comedies, which dealt frivolously with the institution of marriage. The other main class of objections in this field dealt with divorce. Thirteen pictures met with objection because they presented with approval divorce as the answer to the theme's problem; another thirteen contained objectionable treatment of divorce in an approving way.

Other frequent sources of objections were suicide and brutality.

"C" and "B" reasons compared.--There are some subjects which appear on the lists of reasons for condemnation of "C" pictures which are not found on the "B" list; there are some on the "B" list which are not on the "C" list; and there are some on both. What is the basis of the distinction?

It should be noted, first, that "C" films are usually condemned for a complexus of reasons. It is, therefore, difficult ever to assert that this or that reason has been of itself sufficient to merit absolute condemnation.

Secondly, the subjects which appear only on the "C" list are white slavery, venereal disease, the "abortion racket," nudist camps, lesbianism, "debauchery," and the illegal drug trade. The condemnations are all directed toward the use of these subjects as plot material. Excepting venereal disease pictures, which will be discussed later, it may be said that the objection to these subjects is based on the consideration that it is impossible to use them as basic plot material without offensive treatment. The concomitant objections all indicate

that the treatment in each case was, in fact, considered offensive.
The conclusion to be drawn is that it is not the subject matter itself
which is taboo, that the concern is not "so much about the materials
selected for a story as about the moral treatment of those materials."[1]

The reasons which appear only on the "B" list are, principally,
"light treatment of marriage," and approval for divorce, either in
treatment or in solution of the thematic problem. As a matter of fact,
however, the Legion has offered "light treatment of marriage" among
the reasons for condemnation; but the reason does not appear on this
list because these were among the six productions which were first
condemned and then reclassified after they had been revised. The
subject of divorce remains as the outstanding example of a source of
objection to "B" pictures which has never been offered as grounds for
condemning a film outright.

The problem of what to do about pictures which approved of divorce
was raised early in the existence of the Legion of Decency. The
Catholic Church does not recognize the severance of the marital bond
by civil divorce. The Legion, whose policy was shaped by Catholic
Bishops, could not seem to approve of pictures which were considered
apt to encourage an attitude favorable to divorce.

The I.F.C.A., while it was still issuing only lists of recommended
pictures, solved the problem by simply omitting such pictures from its
lists. Mrs. Looram, early in 1935, wrote:

> Since our Church does not approve of pictures that are
> solved by divorce or suicide, we do not recommend such
> pictures, though we do not condemn them. In reference

1. How to judge the morality of motion pictures, p. 8.

to divorce, we appreciate the fact that here in
America a great many of the citizens believe in
divorce and do not find such pictures objectionable.[1]

TABLE 4

REASONS FOR OBJECTION TO ONE HUNDRED AND
FIFTY-SEVEN "B" PICTURES: NOVEMBER,
1939 TO NOVEMBER, 1943

	Theme	Plot	Treatment	Total
Person				
Physical				
Murder	1	0	3	4
Suicide	11	0	5	16
Revenge	1	0	2	3
Mental				
Brutality	0	0	10	10
Hatred	0	0	2	2
Property				
Crime	1	1	3	5
Sex				
Light treatment of				
marriage	3	0	29	32
Divorce	13	0	13	26
Illicit relations	0	2	0	2
"Suggestive" scenes,				
dialogue, etc.	0	0	131	131
Law				
Disrespect for	0	0	1	1
Religion				
Disrespect for	0	0	1	1
Others[a]	1	2	16	19
Total	31	5	217	253

a. Includes lying, dishonesty, "excessive morbidness," and the condoning
of unspecified "immorality" and "wrongdoing."
Sources: Legion of Decency films reviewed, November, 1939-November,
1940; November, 1940-November, 1941; November, 1941-November,
1942; November, 1942-November, 1943.

1. Mrs. James F. Looram, February 14, 1935. Name of addressee confidential.

But when they accepted the task of reviewing films for the Legion of Decency, the I.F.C.A. reviewers were put to the necessity of rating these pictures.

Thus far, any film whose thematic solution involves divorce, or whose treatment approves or condones divorce, has been placed in the "B" category. Some films which have been principally concerned with divorce, have been classified as unobjectionable for adults, e.g., "Marriage is a Private Affair," "The Uncertain Years," and "I Want a Divorce." In these cases the Legion reviewers judged that divorce was being depicted in the proper relation to their standards. That there have been no divorce films in the "C" category is due to the fact, the author has been assured, that thus far no film has been produced which in theme and treatment puts great emphasis upon divorce as the correct solution to marital problems.

There are, finally, reasons which appear on both the "C" and the "B" lists. These include violations of the standards relating to murder, suicide, crime, illicit sex relations, "suggestive" scenes, dialogue, etc., disrespect for law and for religion.

This fact is further confirmation of the assertion that it is not the subject matter, but the way it is handled, which brings forth objection from the Legion.

From the fact that these violations are discovered in both theme and treatment, it can be concluded that the Legion recognizes degrees of objectionableness in both methods of deviating from the accepted standards. Thus, in thematic violations, if the whole burden of a film was that suicide is the acceptable solution to a problem, the film might be condemned. But if suicide was incidental to the solution of the theme's problem, it might be rated "B". In the case of "suggestive" treatment, which is found on both "B" and "C" lists, it also appears that there is a judgment made as to the degree of intensity and the frequency with which the estimated stimuli of sex impulses are presented in the picture.

There are two different sets of judgments involved here. The first is objective: whether or not behavior contrary to the standards is presented as the chief thought content of the picture. The second is subjective: in one case, whether the scene, or costume, or whatever it might be, is apt to excite sexual impulses to a greater or less degree of intensity; or, in another case, whether the audience is likely to be left with the impression, more or less sharp, that deviations from the accepted standards are approved or condoned.

In the cases where the judgments are subjective, i.e. where the reviewer is forced to estimate the "normal" audience reaction on the basis of the reviewer's own reaction, the Legion relies on getting a consensus from a number of reviewers. As an illustration of this, the author may report his own observation. He accompanied three of the Legion staff to the preview of a picture which was about to be released suddenly before the regular Legion reviewers had seen the film. In the picture, a "sympathetic" character participated in blackmail. Recognition of this fact was an objective judgment. Equally objective was the judgment that the act was incidental to the solution of the picture's theme. The question was, then, was the picture's audience likely to leave with the impression that blackmail was the right thing to do? There was disagreement on this point among the reviewers. Faced with this situation, the decision was made to suspend judgment until

more of the reviewers had seen the picture. After reports had come in
from other reviewers, the picture was rated unobjectionable for adults.

In cases, then, where the rating depends upon an estimate of probable
audience reaction, the Legion, in effect, acts upon the assumption that
the larger the sample, the more representative it is apt to be. Theo-
retically, of course, the Legion reviewers are not a random sample,
nor even a strictly representative one. Practically, however, no other
solution is possible, if pictures are to be previewed and classified
at all.

Unpublished Reports on Six "C" Pictures

Between February, 1936, and November, 1943, the Legion of
Decency condemned six productions of major Hollywood companies, each
bearing the seal of the Hays office. All of these pictures were
revised by the producing companies and reclassified by the Legion.
Hence they do not appear on the published annual lists among the "C"
pictures.

The Legion does not lightly condemn a major production. There
are innumerable conferences among the Legion staff, extra showings
are requested, more reviewers are called in, the consultors are
summoned; every possible precaution is taken to make sure that the
action is not hasty or ill-advised. The individual reports on such
pictures, consequently, are worth careful inspection.

In some cases, this study reveals only a more detailed statement
of the same reasons which have previously been noted in the study of
the published reasons. These will be briefly mentioned. In other
cases, there are new insights into the standards upheld by the Legion;

these will be set forth at somewhat greater length. Finally, the last picture to be discussed will offer important evidence concerning the Legion's understanding of the relation between convention and morality; this, since it can be generalized, is the chief finding of this section.

The six condemned pictures were: "Yes, My Darling Daughter" (1939), "Strange Cargo" (1940), "This Thing Called Love" (1941), "Two-Faced Woman" (1941), "White Cargo" (1942), "Lady of Burlesque" (1943). Because the last three named offer little new insight into Legion evaluations, they will be taken up first. These three were condemned principally because of the stimuli they were considered to offer to sex responses from the audience.

"Lady of Burlesque".--Sixteen regular reviewers saw this film, as well as many consultors, of whom only four, however, wrote out ballots. There were fourteen objections to the costumes, thirteen to the dialogue, eleven to the dancing, eight to a song, and six to situations. All of these were considered to be too faithful to the world of burlesque.

"White Cargo".--Film trade papers described the picture as "seduction marathon...sexy, scorching";[1] "extremely provocative";[2] containing "a cooch dance that's more Minsky than Afriko."[3] Twenty-seven Legion reviewers reached similar conclusions. There were twenty-two objections to the seductive gesturings and posturings of the leading female character; fourteen objections to her costume, eleven to the

1. Box office, September 19, 1942.
2. Motion picture daily, September 15, 1942.
3. Variety, September 16, 1942.

dance she performed, five to her alleged mockery of marriage. In
addition, three reviewers objected to the theme, declaring that it
implied the impossibility of overcoming the moral hazards of a
tropical, depraved environment.

"Two-Faced Woman".--Twenty-one reviewers and seven consultors
previewed this picture. There were twenty-one objections that scenes
of love-making were too passionate; twenty-one objections to "suggestive"
dialogue, and seventeen to a costume worn by the leading female
character. Ten made specific objection to the casual treatment of
marriage.

"This Thing Called Love".--This film called for a more careful
examination of values and standards than the three pictures just
mentioned.

The producer's advertisement outlined the plot as follows:

> ...Tice Collins returns to New York to marry
> Ann Winters, who believes that couples should
> make sure they can tolerate each other as persons
> before they can consummate marriage. Ann,...
> persuades Tice that they marry and live together
> in name only for three months. Tice, for his part,
> employs every subterfuge he can think of to make
> his bride relent.

The plot was obviously concocted to provide the chance to show
extensive scenes of seduction which would evade the letter of the
Production Code because the principles were married. Variety noted
this: "It's a 'new' way of skirting around Mr. Breen's frowns."[1] And
Cue's reviewer described the film as "skating skillfully along the thin
edge of the Hays office code."[2] As Bosley Crowther commented some

---

1. Variety, December 25, 1940.
2. Cue, February 14, 1941.

time later:

> Marriages may be made in heaven for one thing, but
> they're made in Hollywood for something else again.
> They're made as a simple expedient to get around
> the restrictions of the Production Code. Much of
> the dialogue and situations in these comedies is
> boldly risque.... The fundamental purpose of these
> pictures is to titillate the audience with a tease.[1]

Of the seventeen reviewers and the thirteen consultors who previewed
the film, twenty objected to the suggestive sequences and dialogues.

The element which distinguishes this picture from the others so
far mentioned was the wife's choice of a trial period of continence
against the wishes of her husband. Fifteen of the objections related
to this aspect of the picture. It was noted that the wife's plan
violated two standards: one according to which marriage should be
entered upon as a permanent union, not subject to trial; the other
according to which legitimate marital rights may not be denied one's
partner. It was further noted that although the theme of the picture
had the wife abandon her plan, it did not suggest any inherent
wrongness in the scheme: her decision was based merely upon her fear
for her husband's fidelity.

"Strange Cargo".--Nineteen of the twenty-three reviewers and
fourteen consultors who previewed this picture objected to suggestive
dialogue and sequences. The film was unusual, however, inasmuch as
the main objection was to certain religious features.

Its plot was built around the escape of a group of convicts,
together with a prostitute, from a prison island. A vaguely defined
character led them out of danger to safety and also led them to repent

---

1. The New York times, November 16, 1941.

of their evil ways.

Two sets of values concerned with religion emerged from the Legion's review of the film. The first of these was the value set upon the Bible: that reverence is due to the writings in the Bible because they are divinely inspired. Nineteen of the objections were directed toward passages in the film which offended in this regard; especially objectionable was a scene in which one of the escaping convicts read aloud to the prostitute a passage from the Old Testament which is used in Catholic liturgy in reference to the Virgin Mother of Christ.

The second set of values was less clearly opposed by the picture. The crucial point was the interpretation intended to be set upon the leader of the convicts, named Cambreau. R. R. Crisler declared in his review of the film: "We do not know who this character Cambreau may be, and we dare not define him, for it is evident that...he is not a natural man."[1] Howard Barnes interpreted the character to be God, but declared the film story "a muddle of moods and treatments."[2]

Many of the Legion reviewers were not clear on the point. But ten of them decided that most audiences would interpret Cambreau to be Jesus Christ. In that event, they considered, the "subjective, emotional experience, without relation to dogma, faith or grace,"[3] depicted in the film, would be taken by the audience to be the religious teachings of the real Christ. This was matter for serious objection.

A complicated set of values was at stake here. The ones most

1. The New York times, April 26, 1940.
2. New York Herald-tribune, April 26, 1940.
3. Consultor's report.

frequently mentioned in the reports were the irrational character of the "religious" experience portrayed in the story, its "naturalism," which implicitly denied the existence of the super-natural order, and the suggestion of pantheism, which denied the transcendence of God.

When the picture was revised, the producer inserted shots which made it clear that Cambreau was a strictly human character. This, together with the elimination of the "suggestive" items and the offensive references to the Bible, lifted the picture, in Legion estimation, into the class "Unobjectionable for Adults."

"Yes, My Darling Daughter".--This was the first major picture to be condemned by the New York reviewers. Sixteen reviewers and fourteen consultors previewed the picture.

Its plot was described thus by the Motion Picture Herald:

> ...depicts the unconventional attitudes and reactions of an extremely modern household to the not essentially modern planning of two young persons anent a prenuptial weekend sans surveillance.[1]

The significant difference between this and the other condemned films is that there were practically no objections to scenes, dialogue or situations as likely to stimulate sex responses in the audience. The objections related to parental authority, to convention and morality, and to the film's attitude toward sex relations.

There were fourteen objections that the defiance of her parents' scruples by "Darling Daughter," together with the mother's weakness in eventually doing "something she feels is wrong, for fear of what the daughter will think of her,"[2] constituted a violation of the accepted standards of parental authority. Ten objected specifically to the lines

----

1. Motion picture herald, February 11, 1939.
2. Reviewer's report.

spoken by the daughter to her mother: "Don't be a hypocrite. It's too late in the day for you to take a moral stand. It's none of your business what I'm doing."

Thirteen objected that the daughter's attitude toward the convention which forbids unmarried couples to spend an unchaperoned weekend together was generalized to include all adherence to convention as "hypocrisy" and "narrow-mindedness." Eight thought the story went further: that by its identification of convention with morality, it showed "a cynical disregard of the existence of objective standards of morality."[1] Five objected specifically to the sequence in which "Darling Daughter" was shown apparently seducing her fiance; they seemed especially concerned with the fact that the girl's taking the initiative made the boy's regard for convention seem the more ridiculous.

Ten objected to the lines of the girl's grandmother, six of them quoting the passage in which she said:

> You know the only thing that puzzles me is why
> the good Lord invented such beautiful things as
> the trees and the flowers and the birds and then
> has to go and invent sex!

These lines were considered to be in opposition to the acceptable attitude, in which sex relations are taken to be good in themselves.

There were, finally, six who objected that the trial weekend bore too close a resemblance to the unacceptable trial marriage concept.

After cuts of some thirteen hundred feet, more than ten minutes of

---

1. Consultor's report.

playing time, had eliminated many of the objectionable lines and
sequences, and had reduced the emphasis upon the attack on convention,
the picture was reclassified "B".

Parental authority.--It may be significant that these reviews of
"Yes, My Darling Daughter" reveal a strongly favorable attitude toward
parental authority. This is in accord with Dinkel's findings, in
which Catholic youths scored higher than Protestant youths in an
attitude test relating to the support of aged parents.[1] Respect for
parental authority and responsibility for aged parents are, as Dinkel
notes, important aspects of family solidarity. This ties in with the
generally favorable attitude of the Legion toward the family as an
institution supported by monogamy, chastity, no divorce, etc. But,
in the case of responsibility for aged parents, Dinkel finds the
Protestant attitude also positive, although not in as high degree as
the Catholic. It may be concluded that the difference between
Protestant and Catholic on this point is not one of opposition, but
of difference in the intensity of the favorable attitude.

Convention and morality.--Undoubtedly the most significant feature
of the Legion's reaction to "Yes, My Darling Daughter" was its reve-
lation of the Legion's attitude toward convention.

In this picture, the "convention" violated was that which demands
chaperonage for young, unmarried couples who spend the night under a
strange roof. The objection was that the film presented such unconventional behavior with approval, inasmuch as it argued against the
parents' scruples and triumphantly demonstrated that the dreaded

---

1. Robert M. Dinkel, "Attitudes of children toward supporting aged
parents," American sociological review, IX (1944), 372.

consequences did not ensue.

The Legion reviewers held that this convention was not obsolescent; that such a story would tend to break down attitudes of respect for this convention. The "pure" intentions of the girl were irrelevant, said one consultor:

> Chaperonage is a convention of society for the safeguard of morals, not only to frustrate deliberate intentions of wrong-doing, but more particularly to protect the young against those circumstances which might lead to unpremeditated violations of morals.[1]

This film, said another consultor, conveys the "false idea to young people that it is easy for two people in love to spend the weekend together without sin."[2]

Implied here is the distinction between convention and morality; that, in some cases, at least, conventions are related to morality, as standards whose violation is an "occasion of sin."

The distinction between "convention" and "morality" is common in Legion of Decency thinking. Most often, although not in this case, it occurs in a context relating to stimuli calculated to excite sexual responses.

Father Parsons, in 1932, had discussed the point with reference to the Production Code:

> In sex questions there are two things sharply to be distinguished. There are certain essential acts, and the thoughts, images and desires connected with them. There are also the conventions we throw around them to protect these acts, etc. Violations of those conventions may or may not be wrong, according as this violation is or is not in

---

1. Consultor's report.
2. Consultor's report.

the nature of a proximate occasion of sin, in
the acts, etc. Curiously, in motion pictures,
plays, books, paintings, it is these proximate
occasions that are chiefly involved. Violation
of them is not always in itself sinful. They
are subject to change as society changes.[1]

Skinner, in the work previously referred to, makes a similar

distinction:

We might say roughly that there are two main
kinds of indecency. One merely offends current
standards of good taste and convention; the
other may actually offend a moral sense. An
illustration of the first kind of so-called
indecency is the matter of style in dress. Any
average community of the year 1900 would have
considered the short skirts of the middle
"twenties" indecent....
    There is another kind of indecency, however,
which relates closely to the old established
Catholic view of the "occasions of sin."...The
mere question of good taste is superseded by
the more important question of the effect of
the particular scenes or dialogue upon the
average audience.[2]

The dividing line between violations of conventions which offend

good taste and violations which may be "occasions of sin" for the

beholder is not always immediately evident. Thus Monsignor McClafferty

had to explain to a dissenting clergymen the rating given by the Legion

to a musical film:

In the Eddie Cantor film to which you referred,
"Ali Baba Goes to Town," the objectionable dialogue
and sequences were more offensive to good taste
than to Catholic moral standards. Our reviewers
resented the vulgarities and a "Minskyesque"
sequence of three colored dancers but did not feel
that it would seriously tempt an audience to sin.[3]

---

1. Wilfrid Parsons, S.J. to Martin Quigley, March 7, 1932.
2. Skinner, op. cit., pp. 5 f.
3. Monsignor McClafferty, February 17, 1938. Name of addressee
   confidential.

In another context, and this was the case with the film under
discussion, the distinction relates to the effect of the behavior in
question, not upon the beholder, but upon the active participants.
If violation of the conventional standard of behavior is held to be a
likely "occasion of sin" for the violators, the unconventional
behavior is considered to be, for that reason, immoral. But if the
violation is held to provide no "occasion of sin," the non-conforming
behavior is considered merely "unconventional," but not "immoral." A
movie which presents "immoral" violations of conventions with
approval, is objected to. It depends, then, upon whether or not the
violation of the convention is held to be generally an "occasion of
sin."

Because different peoples, in different parts of the world,
have different conventions designed to make difficult violations of
the same moral standards, and even in the same locality the conventions
may change over a period of years, Pius XI wrote: "circumstances,
usages and forms vary from country to country, so it does not seem
practical to have a single list for all the world."[1]

Relation of Extrinsic Factors to Legion Values

For the most part, Legion reviewers consider the content of the
movies they see, weighing their conformity with the accepted standards
without consideration for extrinsic factors. However, there are situations in which external factors enter into the value-judgements of
the reviewers; there are, likewise, situations in which the Legion
has decided to disregard them. These final pages on Legion values will

1. On motion pictures, p. 15.

segregate these cases.

Audience Control

The first, and most important of these, is the matter of audience control. The movies are aimed at mass audiences. Since the fundamental assumption underlying all the Legion's activity is that certain kinds of pictures have an adverse moral effect on at least some of the people who see them, there must be involved some estimate of the mental and moral caliber of the audience. The two main considerations are the age composition of the audience, and its social environment.

Age composition of audience.--The first question to be considered is whether all motion pictures must be tailored to fit the requirements of the sub-adult section of the audience.

The Production Code had considered this problem. In the "Reasons Supporting" the particular applications it states: "Maturer minds may easily understand and accept without harm subject matter in plots which do younger people positive harm." The Code thereupon recommended the creation of a special type of theater, catering exclusively to adult audiences, for "plays with problem themes, difficult discussions and maturer treatment."

The economic structure of the film industry operates to prevent the audience limitation inherent in the "adult theater" plan. This problem, therefore, was much to the fore during the Legion of Decency campaign in 1934. Fear that the Legion would be satisfied only with film suitable for twelve-year olds was quickly mollified by the publication of a letter from Archbishop McNicholas to Will Hays. The

113

Archbishop said:

> One recognizes that there are legitimate dramatic
> values in life, affording themes of proper and
> profound interest to mature minds, which would be
> utterly unfit for the impressionable minds of
> youth. Those who have thought the problem through
> are convinced that many pictures should bear
> approval for adult patronage, while others could well
> be approved for general patronage.[1]

Legion reviewers follow this line, dividing "unobjectionable"
movies into those "unobjectionable for general patronage," and those
"unobjectionable for adults."

No attempt has been made to set a hard and fast line of demar-
cation between the age groups above and below the border line. The
"ability to comprehend adult problems and to view and measure them
against a proper and balanced psychological and philosophical
background" is the quality Legion reviewers have in mind when they
make the distinction.[2]

Social environment of audience.--Consideration of another factor
influencing movie audiences has resulted in the Legion's placing
certain pictures in the condemned, "C" category. These are pictures
presenting the effects, cure and social aspects of venereal disease.

Most of these films have been condemned for their sensational
treatment of the subject, using the plot as a subterfuge for
presenting series of objectionable sequences.

Certain films of this nature, however, have presented the subject
with inoffensive treatment. The first picture of this sort to be
rated by the Legion was "Damaged Goods," in 1937. The first judgement

---

1. "Report," p. 405.
2. Monsignor McClafferty, April 13, 1938. Name of addressee confiden-
    tial.

of the Legion was that it was "unobjectionable for adults." Further
consideration, however, led to the decision that it was unsuitable for
indiscriminate exhibition. When it was learned that the picture was
booked for general theatrical distribution, the Board of Consultors of
the Legion decided to condemn the film as entertainment material.

The reasoning behind this decision was based upon concern for the
effect of the immediate social environment upon the attitudes and
reactions of the movie audience. The Legion maintains that an
audience whose social character is partially determined by the fact
that both sexes are gathered together to be entertained is not properly
receptive to instruction in sex hygiene. Archbishop McNicholas, after
a similar condemnation of "No Greater Sin," in 1941, stated:

> The motion picture theater is not a clinic; nor
> is it a doctor's consultation room or a classroom.
> It is not the sanctum of the minister of religion;
> nor is it the sanctuary of the home.
> Sex instruction does not come within the function
> of the motion picture theater. On the contrary, to
> assume this grave responsibility would be a perversion
> of the principal function of the theater. Instead of
> rendering any real service to the public welfare, the
> influence thus exercised must be progressively
> degenerating in the moral order.[1]

With reference to the film "To the People of the United States,"
a venereal disease movie produced with the cooperation of Walter Wanger
and the United States Public Health Service, Legion authorities
stated: "The Legion without reservations, qualifications or
conditions takes the position that sex-hygiene films are not suitable
for exhibition in the entertainment motion picture theater."[2]

---

1. Quoted, America, LXVI (October 18, 1941), 40.
2. "Confidential memorandum to dioceses and diocesan organizations of
   the Legion of Decency," September 21, 1944.

Somewhat different was the Legion's action in regard to two
documentary films concerned with child-birth. The Legion did not
condemn these; it placed them in the category "Separately Classified."

Of the first, "Birth of a Baby," in 1938, the Legion stated:

> Intrinsically the film is moral in theme....
> Nevertheless, in forming an integral evaluation
> of the film, external factors must be taken into
> consideration....This production has considerable
> merit from the medical, educational, social and
> technical points of view; however, the film is
> not suited to general exhibition in the theatre,
> where audiences are composed of both sexes and
> various ages, backgrounds, mentalities and temperaments.[1]

Of "The Fight for Life," in 1940, the Legion said:

> Although the film may be considered as possessing
> medical, social and educational value, the intro-
> duction of this type of subject material on the
> theatrical screen for presentation to unselected
> audiences is questionable.[2]

The condemnation of venereal disease pictures reflects the
judgment that the environment of the commercial movie theater would
have an adverse effect upon the value judgments of those who come
to be entertained and witness such films.[3]

The separate classification of the films dealing with childbirth
shows that the Legion does not consider such presentation harmful to
morals. It does manifest a concern for the preservation of a
reverential attitude toward "this subject which is so sacred, private
and personal."[4]

---

1. Quoted in "Report to the Episcopal Committee on Motion Pictures"
   (unpublished), 1938.
2. Ibid., 1940.
3. Cf. M. Sherif, The psychology of social norms, New York, Harper and
   Brothers, 1936.
4. "Report to the Episcopal Committee," 1938.

Advertising

Another extrinsic factor which has affected the rating of at least one picture was the type of advertising used to exploit the film. "Wajan," released in 1938, depicts the daily, ceremonial and religious life of the natives of the Island of Bali. It was first given the rating "unobjectionable for adults," on the condition that the advertising and exploitation conform to the Advertising Code of the Hays office. The exhibitors, however, advertised the picture as if it were sensational and lurid.[1] The Legion thereupon withdrew its "unobjectionable" rating.

Personnel of Cast

The Legion's policy is to judge each film separately, without regard for the past performances of players in the cast, or for their personal activities.

Mae West, whose films had been the target of a special criticism in 1933 and 1934, occasioned some problems in this regard. Her picture "Klondike Annie," early in 1936, was rated "B" by the Legion in spite of her previous record.

Again, in December, 1938, the same Mae West took part in a radio boradcast which gave widespread offense. Three days later the Legion staff was reviewing her picture "Every Day's a Holiday." The picture was rated unobjectionable for adults. Criticized for this action, Mrs. Looram pointed out that the Legion's responsibility was "to judge a film on the merits of the film itself."[2]

---

1. Fortune, XVIII (December, 1938), 71 ff., reproduces some of the advertising matter used to exploit "Wajan."
2. Mrs. James F. Looram, March 2, 1938. Name of addressee confidential.

Esthetic Values

Two other important problems of value discrimination have arisen
in the course of the Legion's history. The first of these was
concerned with esthetics. The other had to do with political values.

In 1936, beginning in February and ending in October, the New
York office of the Legion issued, at irregular intervals, a series
of "Special Estimates," whose purpose was to appraise the entertainment and artistic value of selected pictures. The Episcopal
Committee frowned upon this activity. Archbishop McNicholas wrote
to New York: "The Episcopal Committee never thought of going beyond
the domain of morality."[1] Since that time the Legion has passed no
judgment on the esthetic qualities of the films it has reviewed.

This policy was attacked by Martin Turnell in the English Catholic
monthly, Blackfriars. Turnell expressed his preference for the policy
of the Belgian Catholic Centre of Cinematographic Action:

> The fact that it has carefully considered the
> artistic value of films seems to me to have made
> its work immeasurably more important than the work
> of the Legion of Decency.[2]

Whatever the thoughts of the Bishops may have been regarding the
esthetic level of the films, they made no issue of the matter in their
communications of 1934 enumerating their complaints against the movies.
When they accepted the reorganized Production Code Administration as
the industry's response to their challenge, they knew that it had no
competence to deal with the esthetic qualities of the movies. It
must be concluded that the failure to consider esthetic values is of

----

1. Archbishop McNicholas to Monsignor Edward R. Moore, November 11, 1936.
2. "Cinema in society," Blackfriars, XIX (1938), 582.

deliberate intent.

Political Values

The last problem is that of the Legion's attitude toward the extrinsic factor of political values.

It is probably impossible to delimit with precision the field of politics from all other fields of human activity. Merriam has pointed out that "only confusion will be created by trying to draw too sharp and exclusive a line between political and all other forms of organization."[1] The main reason for this, he says, is that "the political association has a generality of purpose, falling to no other group in so broad a fashion."[2]

Fortunately for the purpose of this study, the problem which arose to face the Legion of Decency in this field was narrow in scope, although peculiarly complicated. The instances have all been concerned with those political values which are involved in the proposed reorganization of society along the lines advocated by the followers of Karl Marx. There was the case of films produced in the Soviet Union under the control of a government which was officially committed to Marxism. There was the case of a film which favored the "Loyalist" faction in the recent Spanish Civil War, when that faction was thought to be of the same mind as the ruling group in the Soviet Union. There was the prospect of Hollywood films with a social message thought likely to be pro-Marxist. And finally, there was the pro-Soviet film, "Mission to Moscow."

---

1. Charles E. Merriam, Political power, New York, Whittlesey House, McGraw-Hill Book Company, 1934, p. 9.
2. Ibid.; cf. Timasheff, Sociology of law, pp. 196-200.

Soviet films.--The films produced in Soviet Russia occasioned only a minor problem. They have usually been exhibited only in the smaller theaters in the largest centers of population. As long as this was the case, the pictures were reviewed, but it was the general policy not to list them in the ratings. The Legion received no requests from its followers for guidance with regard to these films. Since the war began there have been a very few Soviet-made films distributed through major distributors for release through the usual channels. These receive general patronage. The Legion has rated and listed these as it would any other films.

"Blockade".--Greater concern was manifested over the Legion's way of handling the film "Blockade." Walter Wanger produced this picture in the early part of 1938, when a civil war was being fought on the soil of Spain, and simultaneously in the forums of American controversy. The film broke Hollywood precedent by openly favoring one of the Spanish factions, known as the "Loyalists." Catholic opinion in the United States at the time was predominantly anti-Loyalist, principally because some of the Spanish Loyalists had engaged in violent anti-religious activity, and also because the Loyalists were thought to be Marxist-minded, and because they were favored by pro-Marxists in Soviet Russia and elsewhere.

The Legion faced a thorny dilemma. If it should rate the picture as unobjectionable, it would seem to some to countenance support for a group which was connected with immoral doctrines and practices. If it should condemn the film, it would seem to others to be rating the picture on the basis of political, rather than moral values.

To escape this dilemma, the expedient was devised by which the film was given no moral rating at all. It was listed under the caption "separately classified." Attached was the observation: "Many people will regard this picture as containing foreign political propaganda in favor of one side in the present unfortunate struggle in Spain."[1]

By this device the Legion considered that it kept political values from its ratings. But its action was vigorously attacked, nevertheless. Box Office charged it with "certainly departing from its moral estimates of films."[2] Film Survey, organ of the avowedly "anti-fascist" Associated Film Audiences, said:

> No longer is the Legion of Decency the mere watch-dog of decency. It is the self-appointed censor of a nation's progressive ideals. It brings to the movie the standard of narrow suppression, which from time immemorial has fought and blocked all forms of civilized progress.[3]

Marxism in Hollywood.--The controversy quickly carried over into a broader field. It will be remembered that this was the height of the period when the charge and counter-charge of "fascist" and "communist front" echoed in the literature and on the lecture platforms of the United States. Hollywood actors and actresses at this time discovered social theory. Hollywood authors yearned to write scripts with social significance.[4] Legion heads became alarmed at the prospect of Marxism in the movies. Archbishop McNicholas issued a

---

1. Films reviewed, November, 1937-November, 1938, p. 30.
2. Box office, September 24, 1938.
3. Film survey, August, 1938; quoted in "Report to the Episcopal Committee," 1938.
4. Cf. Eugene Lyons, The red decade, Indianapolis, The Bobbs-Merrill Company, 1941, pp. 284-295.

public statement which said:

> The Legion views with grave apprehension those
> efforts now being made to utilize the cinema for
> the spread of ideas antagonistic, not only to
> traditional Christian morality, but to all religion.
> It must oppose the efforts of those who would make
> motion pictures an agency for the dissemination of
> the false, atheistic, and immoral doctrines
> repeatedly condemned by all accepted moral teachers.[1]

On the basis of this statement, the author of the comments on film

censorship in The Yale Law Journal,drew the conclusion that the Legion's

"proper plane is not wholly one of morality."[2] Thorp has taken the

statement to be proof that the handling of "Blockade" "marked a change

in the Legion's policy. 'Communism' is no longer to be ignored but

openly combated."[3]

"Mission to Moscow".--The 1939 Hitler-Stalin pact cleared the air

of charges based on the "Communist--Fascist" dichotomy. But in 1943,

with the Soviet Union very much in the war against Germany, the same

old problem arose once more. This time it was the film version of the

highly controversial book Mission to Moscow which raised the issue.

The book and the picture painted the Soviet Union in glowing colors.

There was, however, no glorification of the Soviet doctrines and

practices which the Legion held to be immoral. In this respect, the

situation was parallel to that which had involved "Blockade."

This time the Legion rated the picture "Unobjectionable for

Adults," adding this observation:

> This film represents the personal observations
> and opinions of ex-Ambassador Joseph E. Davies as
> expressed in his book Mission to Moscow, upon which

---

1. Press release, August 22, 1938.
2. Yale law journal, p. 107.
3. Thorp, op. cit., p. 213.

the film is based. The film in its sympathetic
portrayal of the governing regime in Russia makes
no reference to the anti-religious philosophy and
policy of said regime.[1]

While the picture was widely criticized, as the book had been, for

alleged distortions of fact, the Legion was not criticized for intro-

ducing political values into its ratings. Indeed, the most widely

publicized objection to the Legion's rating came from an editorial in

a Catholic paper, The Herald Citizen of Milwaukee, which the Hearst

paper in Boston quoted as saying:

> It seems to us that in instances such as this
> inexcusable distortion of facts the Legion might
> well have added a frank warning that, though
> unobjectionable for adults as decency goes,
> "Mission to Moscow" is by no means highly moral,
> in the sense that deception is not moral. To
> guard people against indecent movies is a very
> laudable enterprise. But it is important, too,
> to warn them against lies, historical, scientific,
> political,...[2]

Analysis of problem.--It is not the business of this study to

decide whether or not the Legion ought to admit political values into

its ratings. The relevant questions are restricted to those aspects of

the situation which have created the problem, the probable effect of a

policy which would include political values as a partial basis for

evaluation of films, and the actual policy of the Legion.

First, the problem of discriminating political from moral values

has arisen out of a concrete situation in which an existing political

regime, that of the Soviet Union, is identified with doctrines and

---

1. Films reviewed, November, 1942-November, 1943, p. 20.
2. Boston evening American, June 8, 1943.

practices which are considered immoral. Objection to such doctrines and practices need not involve reference to political values. On the other hand, confusion easily arises when the activities of such a regime, or those of its imitators or admirers are evaluated. Because certain doctrines and practices meet with objection, any favorable portrayal of the regime may be considered immoral. Conversely, when reviewers object to the doctrines or practices considered immoral, some may take this action to be objection to the regime as a political institution.

Second, the Legion has some millions of followers ready to accept its assessment of the morality of the behavior portrayed in the movies. It has equipped itself with reviewers and consultors competent in this sphere. It is not clear, however, that its followers are ready to accept its judgment as to the worth of competing systems of political organizations, except insofar as one or the other may be a system which is in itself immoral. Nor is it clear that its followers are ready to accept its decision as to the relative merits of groups who are competing for political power. The Legion is not staffed with political scientists, nor with on-the-spot observers of contemporary political activity throughout the world.

Conceivably, should the Legion elect to make such judgments as those just indicated, judgments based on political values, it might retain the support of its followers. In that case it would continue to function effectively. But if it should fail to gain support for its political judgments, it would run the risk of losing the confidence of its followers in its moral judgments, and would soon cease to exercise its influence in that sphere.

Lastly, as to the actual policy of the Legion as manifested thus far in its existence, this may be said. The statement of Archbishop McNicholas in 1938 was aimed at immoral doctrines, not at a system of political organization. It did not, therefore, signify the adoption of a new policy which would invade the political sphere. In the case of "Blockade," however, the Legion set to one side a picture which was not alleged to portray objectionable behavior or ideas or doctrines. It did this because the film was sympathetic to a political group which included men who were identified with objectionable doctrines and practices. Had the Legion continued this policy, it would have opened the way for the introduction of purely political judgments into its ratings. The fact that "Mission to Moscow" was evaluated like any other picture, not set to one side as "separately classified," indicates that the Legion has realized the dangers inherent in the previous policy, and that it has no intention of assuming the task of political judgment.

CHAPTER IV

MEANS USED BY THE LEGION OF DECENCY

Introduction

Throughout the foregoing analysis of the structure and the ends
of the Legion of Decency, three stages of development have appeared.
Once the Production Code was accepted by the film industry, there was
the stage in which the attempt was made to create pressure through
individual ethical leaders for the enforcement of its provisions.
This stage was followed by that of the Legion of Decency campaign
under the direction of organized ethical leadership. The final stage
of development is that of the permanent functioning of the Legion as it
has been constituted for the past ten years.

Analysis of the means used by the Legion will follow the same
stages of the developmental process: the emergence, the formation
and the permanent functioning of the Legion.

In the beginning of such an analysis, it is necessary to define
the situation which existed when the process of emergence began.
For the means of social action are those elements of the total situation
over which the agent has exercised some control.[1] Empirically they are
discovered through observation of the changes in the initial situation
which the agent has brought about in conformity with his end. The
elements of the situation over which such control is not exercised are
the "conditions" of the action process.[2]

_____

1. Parsons, Structure of social action, p. 44.
2. Ibid.

The Situation

Before the introduction of the Production Code, the relevant
aspects of the motion picture situation were as follows. The film
industry was centralized, organized in the Motion Picture Producers
and Distributors of America, Inc. The movies were a mass medium of
entertainment, aimed at the widest possible, unselected audience. The
films being produced were to an undefined extent regarded as
endangering the values embodied in the ideal patterns of society.
Informal control was ineffective. Formal public control was confined
to scattered, local efforts of official censorship bodies. Private
control was being exercised by certain groups engaged in the "praise
the best, ignore the rest" activity. And there was a limited amount
of self-control being exercised by the industry through the Hays office.
The net effect of the formal controls was regarded as unsatisfactory.

Conditions of the action process.--Out of this total situation,
certain elements were accepted throughout the Legion process as
"conditions" which the Legion did not attempt to change. These were,
first, the centralized structure of the industry, and, second, the
practice of producing movies for mass audiences.

Industry self-control was another element of the situation which
was also accepted as a condition of its action by the Legion, insofar
as there was never, during any part of the process, any attempt to
eliminate it.

However, insofar as the Legion action process was directed toward
a future state of affairs in which industry self-control would be
changed in the direction of more effective operation, effective self-
regulation was an end of the Legion. It was only an intermediate end,

hence the means to a further end, the preservation of the values described in the previous chapter.

Maintenance of the system of self-regulation was, then, a condition of Legion activity. Changes within that system, in the direction of greater efficiency, were a means to the ultimate end.

In summary, the Legion accepted a centralized industry, the production of pictures for mass audiences, and the self-control of the Hays office as the conditions within the limits of which it would select means to its end.

Means Used in the Process of Emergence

The process of emergence began with the introduction of the Production Code into the total situation. This was the initial, crucial event. The Legion emerged as a pressure group exercising constraint upon those who had the power to enforce conformity with the Code. The place of the Code in the self-regulatory process calls for some explanation in order to understand why social pressure was needed to enforce it.

The Production Code

Technical and ethical norms.--A code of standards is a set of rules which provides normative guidance in making the choice of appropriate means.[1] Usually such norms are classified as technical, ethical or legal in character.[2] The distinction between legal norms

1. Parsons, op. cit., p. 44.
2. Timasheff, Sociology of law, pp. 79 ff. Cf. Parsons, op. cit., pp. 649 ff. Rules of good taste are not considered here. For discussions of such rules, see Timasheff, op. cit., pp. 147-154, and Parsons, op. cit., pp. 679-681.

and all others is founded on the objective criterion that only legal norms are supported by the organized power of the state.[1] The difference between ethical and technical norms, however, is founded on a subjective criterion: the mode in which the rule is apprehended by the agent. The same rule may be accepted by one as a technical rule, and by another as an ethical rule. Thus, "be honest" is an ethical rule for many; for others it expresses merely the "best policy," and is only a technical rule.

Both ethical and technical rules belong to the same genus, inasmuch as both impose some sort of constraint upon those who accept them. The specific difference between them is located in the kind of constraint imposed. The constraint imposed by ethical rules is categorical, based on the apprehension that they are means to an end which "ought" to be attained. The constraint imposed by technical rules is hypothetical, based on the apprehension that they are means to ends which one is free to elect or to reject.[2]

Original ethical character of the Code.--The original formulators of the Production Code considered it to be a set of ethical norms. Several factors point to this conclusion.

Martin Quigley said that he had intended:

> a detailed exposition,...of the philosophy involved in the subject of public entertainment. This seemed to be the first need, and to this there seemed to be reason for adding a detailed and clearcut explanation of the moral grounds governing the several principal questions involved.[3]

1. Timasheff, op. cit., pp. 263 ff.
2. Ibid., p. 81.
3. Letter, Martin Quigley to Joseph I. Breen, February 21, 1938.

Inspection of the original formulation of the Code bears this out.[1] The first several pages of the original document develop at length the theme that there is an ethical obligation to society involved in the production of motion pictures. And further on in the Code, when specific rules are formulated, there is always an attempt to show that the rule is derived from some ethical principle. A large proportion of the document is devoted to the didactic purpose of teaching the existence and the character of the ethical obligations at stake.

Furthermore, the Code was presented to the producers without effort to pressure them into acceptance. Plans to present the Code as a demand from the church group, or, alternatively, to get the film executives in New York to pressure the producers into accepting it, were rejected. It was decided that a set of regulations arbitrarily imposed upon the producers from outside would not stand as good a chance of being observed as would a set of regulations which had been discussed and agreed upon by the men who were to observe them.

When, therefore, the producers affixed their signatures to the Code, February 17, 1930, it was reasonable to conclude that they were expressing their direct recognition of the ethical standards expressed in it.

Indications of technical character of the Code.--Certain developments occurred during the process of gaining the producers' acceptance of the Code which had the effect of diluting its ethical character, and of introducing certain aspects of a purely technical character.

---

1. The Code in its original form is quoted in full, Martin, op. cit., pp. 271-284.

The first of these was the insertion of the "Don'ts" and the "Be Carefuls" into the text. These were, as has been noted, a set of rules based on a study of the deletions and revisions demanded by various official censors.[1] They were proposed as a set of technical rules, conformity to which would minimize difficulties with the censors. Insertion of them into the Code introduced provisions regarding such matters as "the use of liquor in American life," "miscegenation," "offense to national feelings," and numerous "repellent subjects." The link between particular rules and ethical principles, which had been the chief feature of the original document, was in the case of such rules as these either very tenuous or altogether non-existent. Since the producers had known these as technical rules, their inclusion with the others could easily lead them to bring the whole Code down from the ethical to the technical level.

The second development was that of bringing the "Don'ts" and "Be Carefuls," and other "particular applications," to the foreground of the document, relegating the didactic and explanatory portions of the Code to the subordinate position of "Reasons Supporting" the particular rules.

The third development was the virtual suppression, by the Hays office, of the ethical portion of the Code. Not for many years were the "Reasons Supporting" included in the versions of the Code published by the Hays office.

These developments tended to lessen the commitment of the producers to a categorically binding set of ethical norms.

_____

1. Supra, p. 18.

The enforcement procedure adopted by the producers in 1930 also gave indications that the Code was being considered as merely technical rules.

The "Resolution for Uniform Interpretation" read in part:

> 1. When requested by production managers, the Association of Motion Picture Producers, Inc., shall secure any facts, information or suggestions concerning the probable reception of stories or the manner in which in its opinion they may best be treated.
> 2. That each production manager may submit in confidence a copy of each or any script to the Association of Motion Picture Producers, Inc. The Association...will give... confidential advice and suggestions...designating wherein in its judgment the script departs from the provisions of the Code, or wherein from experience or knowledge it is believed that exception will be taken to the story or treatment.[1]

Significantly, the judgment of the reviewing body was not to be confined to putative violations of the Code, but was to give its opinion as to the "probable reception" of the script, especially as to the likelihood that "exception will be taken" to it. Again, these are technical, not ethical judgments. It is as if the Code were understood to say, "If you want to avoid trouble, make your pictures this way." If such rules are violated, and no trouble ensues, they cease to be effective regulations, even of a technical character.

A second significant feature of the enforcement machinery was the procedure prescribed for appealing from adverse decisions. The "Resolution for Uniform Interpretation" provided for compulsory submission of finished pictures for judgment as to its conformity with the Code. In the event of adverse decisions, the producer was given the right to appeal from such decisions to "the Production Committee"

---

1. Production code and uniform interpretation, Motion Picture Producers and Distributors of America, Inc., n.d., p. 7.

of the Association of Producers. The Production Committee was a
standing committee of producers, three members of which were to be
designated in rotation to serve as a jury to pass judgment on these
appeals.

The producer making such appeal would have a large financial
interest in its result. But because he, in his turn, will be on the
jury to judge his fellow-producer's product, he is in a position to
exert substantial pressure upon his jury to be lenient toward his
product so that when his turn comes he will be lenient toward theirs.
A jury, under such circumstances, is not likely to render free and
independent judgment.

The net result of the developments regarding the text of the
Code, and of the procedure adopted to enforce the Code was that the
Code was to a great extent reduced to the level of technical rules,
and that enforcement of these rules was lodged in the persons of
those who were very likely to be subject to the same "bombardment
of interests"[1] which produced the violations of the rules.

In such a situation the use of some sanctions to enforce
conformity to the rules becomes an imperative adjunct to the control
process.

Pressure Through Individual Ethical Leaders

The sponsors of the Code defined the situation correctly. To
meet the needs of the situation, they sought to create social pressure
in favor of conformity with the Code.

The nature of social pressure is explained by Timasheff.[2] It is

1. Parsons, op. cit., p. 402.
2. Timasheff, op. cit., pp. 105 ff.

rooted in attitudes hostile to violations of the accepted ideal
patterns. Explanations of the origin of these hostile attitudes may
vary, but the fact of their existence is not controverted. Folsom
puts it thus: "When a value is directly attacked, or is ignored under
circumstances calling it to attention, those who hold the value are
resentful."[1]

To create pressure which would force the producers to conform to
the Code, it was necessary to foster attitudes which would be hostile
to violations of the Code. That meant, in the minds of the advocates
of the Code, that the Code would have to be built up as a positive
value.

To this end was directed all the activity which resulted in the
statements of approval from individual ethical leaders, cited in the
second chapter.[2]

That this means of creating social pressure was ineffective is
demonstrated by the fact that plenty of non-conformity with the Code
was still in evidence when the Legion campaign opened in 1934. The
following reasons for this lack of success may be adduced.

First, the fact that the campaign of the Legion in 1934 met with
such a quick response from the public indicates that an educational
campaign designed to build up the Code as a positive value was
unnecessary. The provisions of the Code, being an application of the
most fundamental precepts of a generally accepted ethical system,
needed no promotion to secure their recognition. It was as unnecessary

---

1. Joseph K. Folsom, "Changing values in sex and family relations,"
   American sociological review, II (1937), 719.
2. Supra, p. 41-44.

as trying to create a favorable attitude toward the Ten Commandments.

Second, social pressure manifests itself when violations of the accepted norms are either imminent or actual. During "normal" periods it is latent.[1] But the activity of this period was not directed toward creating social awareness of the fact that the Code was being violated. Violations were not called to the public's attention.

Finally, social pressure exists as a social force only when the hostile attitudes in which it is rooted are translated into overt action. Violators do not feel the pressure of attitudes through a process of intuition; they feel pressure when and insofar as they become the targets of hostile social action. This action takes the form of social sanctions.[2] But during this period no concrete forms of action, no sanctions were presented or suggested to the people. Even if the people were aware of the violations, they could not exert social pressure by saying, "Too bad, but what can you do about it?"

The positive accomplishments of this stage were few, but as part of a trial and error process it was important. During this period it was definitely established that the producers would not conform to the Code without strong pressure from outside their own ranks. Most important, it was learned that the technique of creating social pressure by securing laudatory statements about the Code from individual ethical leaders was deficient.

This knowledge played its part in the decision to enlist the support of an organized group of ethical leaders, and in determining

1. Timasheff, op. cit., p. 106.
2. Ibid., p. 108.

the means adopted by the pressure group which those leaders instituted.

Two minor attempts to create pressure took place just before the end of this period, however, and they must be briefly noticed. These efforts were tangential to the total process; they did not lead directly into the next phase.

In the first, bankers in the East, with financial interests in the film industry, were urged to put pressure on the producers to conform to the Code. This attempt did not bring the desired results, whether because the bankers did not accept the standards of the Code as normative guidance for business activity, or because they were not in a position to demand, and get, conformity from the producers.

In the second, an effort was made to have the Production Code included in the N.R.A. code for the movie industry. The government would thus have stood ready to use its power to enforce the system of self-regulation. The Production Code was not included as such in the N.R.A. code. In any case enforcement of N.R.A. code was generally ineffective, and the whole procedure was soon declared unconstitutional.

Means Used in the Process of Formation

In the functionally differentiated structure which took shape during the process of formation, the Episcopal Committee determined matters of policy, the local Bishops recruited the following, and the following exerted social pressure on the movie industry.

The Episcopal Committee

The principal policy-making decisions of the Episcopal Committee were: (1) to recruit a pressure group; (2) to propose a buyers' strike as a sanction; (3) to direct the pressure towards more efficient operation of industry self-regulation.

The first two of these policies will be treated under the functioning of the local Bishops and of the following. The last policy, to be placed in its proper perspective, must be considered in the light of the several alternative policies which were presented to the Episcopal Committee.

Elimination of motion picture entertainment.--Speculatively, the Episcopal Committee could have tried to direct the pressure towards the total elimination of the movies as factors in the entertainment world. Such an attempt would have been analogous to the attempt to outlaw the production of alcoholic beverages embodied in the drive for prohibition. That this possibility received no serious consideration was due to the fact that among the norms guiding the Committee's choice of means was the Catholic tradition which recognizes entertainment as a "natural" need of mankind.[1]

Enactment of legislation for governmental control.--At the time the Episcopal Committee was formulating its policy, i.e., during the period between November, 1933, when it was appointed, and April, 1934, when it announced the Legion of Decency, its attention was drawn by the Federal Motion Picture Council to the Patman Bill then before Congress.[2] The Bill provided for a law which would forbid interstate

1. Supra, pp. 75 f.
2. Letter, Wm. Sheafe Chase to Archbishop McNicholas, April 2, 1934.

carriage to movies which had been judged to violate the Production
Code by a commission of five men and four women to be appointed by the
President of the United States.[1]

In the latter part of 1934, Mrs. Robbins Gilman, motion picture
chairman of the National Congress of Parents and Teachers, toured
fifteen states urging complete government control over the movies.

Mrs. Gilman's objective was to take over the film industry, not
as it was then constituted,

> but under a different management and production
> policy, and use it for the free recreation of
> the public in civic centers and public auditoriums.[2]

Motion picture content was to be completely controlled by a non-
industry group:

> The motion picture industry should be taken
> from the hands of the Hollywood moguls and turned
> over to professional educators....A national Board
> of Education should be created and should have
> complete responsibility for the content of all
> films of the recreational type.[3]

The Board was evidently to be a governmental creation:

> The governments of Russia, Germany, Italy and
> France have made remarkable progress in film
> production. They recognize the value of the
> cinema to education. They accept the responsi-
> bility also of protecting their citizens from
> being misrepresented, through their films, to
> other peoples. This is a government function.[4]

The Episcopal Committee had already chosen its policy at the

---

1. U.S. 73d Congress, H. 6097, The Patman Bill, "To provide for
   inspecting, classifying, and cataloguing motion pictures, both
   silent and talking, before they enter interstate or foreign commerce,
   to create a federal motion picture commission, to define its powers,
   and for other purposes."
2. Washington star, November 4, 1934.
3. Philadelphia Inquirer-public ledger, November 6, 1934.
4. The New York times, November 9, 1934.

time of Mrs. Gilman's tour, but the norms which led it to reject support
for federal censorship were valid a fortiori for rejection of the
totalitarian Gilman plan.

The norms which operated in the decision not to use its pressure
in favor of the Patman Bill were both ethical and technical. Ethically,
the Committee asserted privately that it did not favor federal censorship because of its concern about "the growing notion of the State's
right to supremacy in the realm of moral teaching." Technically, as a
norm of efficiency, the Committee expressed its unwillingness to have
"interpretations of the regulatory provisions left to political
appointees, subject to political pressure."[1]

Archbishop McNicholas published this statement:

> Public opinion, if governed by good sense and
> relentless in its opposition to the evil motion
> picture, has many advantages over censorship, which
> may be politically controlled or corrupted or may
> become utterly indifferent to the commonweal.[2]

Abolition of certain trade practices.--The trade practices then
prevalent in the motion picture industry included those known as
block-booking and blind selling.[3] Distributors sold pictures by the
block, i.e., a number of pictures were sold simultaneously in a
group so that the exhibitor had to buy all or none of the block. This
was block-booking. Along with this practice went the practice of
selling pictures sight unseen, often before they were even produced.

---

1. "Notes," (mimeographed) sent to Bishops by the Episcopal Committee,
   May 16, 1934, p. 7.
2. "The Episcopal Committee and the problem of evil motion pictures,"
   Ecclesiastical review, XCI (1934), 116. Quoted in The New York times,
   July 25, 1934.
3. These practices are described in detail in The motion picture industry--
   a pattern of control, pp. 23-34.

This was blind selling.

Many thought that the elimination of these practices would improve the moral level of movies by giving the exhibitor greater freedom of choice in selecting his attractions, thus giving him the opportunity of respecting the preferences of his patrons for unobjectionable films. Independent exhibitors have consistently opposed the practices for financial and competitive reasons.

The Patman Bill proposed legislation to outlaw these practices. The Motion Picture Research Council also advocated legislation to obtain the same end.[1]

The Episcopal Committee refused to champion such legislation. The principal norm governing this choice seems to have been one of efficiency; partially the choice was governed by the same norms which dictated opposition to federal censorship.

The clearest statement of these norms came two years later, when the Episcopal Committee refused to support the Pettingill Bill which proposed to abolish these practices.[2] The Committee stated that reasons of efficiency had led it to direct its activities along a single channel; that the attack on block-booking should be handled by local groups.

> The National Legion of Decency has not dealt with the exhibitor, but with the producer. To deal with the former would mean conducting the campaign on 12,000 fronts rather than confining it to one front-- the producers.
> Block booking has a business side and a moral side.... The Legion has not dealt with questions that have not at

1. The New York times, March 4, 1934, March 22, 1934, April 19, 1934, October 5, 1934.
2. U. S. 74th Congress, S. 3012, The Neeley-Pettingill Bill, "To prohibit and to prevent the trade practices known as 'compulsory block booking' and 'blind selling' in the leasing of motion picture films in interstate and foreign countries."

> least a moral implication. Block booking,
> however, as it involves a moral question--that is,
> the forced acceptance of salacious pictures--should
> be dealt with. Local groups, in such cases, should
> sustain the exhibitor not merely by protesting, but
> in any legal action taken against the producer....[1]

Further, the likelihood of political control was envisaged, and a

policy which led in that direction was unwelcome.

> The Legion of Decency sees in legislative
> measures not a means of securing a wholesome screen,
> but rather a grave danger of political censorship.
> One law may lead to another.[2]

Private censorship.--There was precedent for setting up a private

board of censors, with authority to reject and revise films. The

National Board of Censorship of Motion Pictures had been just such an

agency. During the Legion campaign, Rabbi Goldstein advocated setting

up a somewhat similar board.[3] Such a group, as he expressed it later,

would have "the authority to supervise the selection of themes and the

approval of pictures in the name of the public."[4] It would appoint and

supervise an executive staff to enforce the Production Code. It would

be composed of "representatives of the industry, education and the

ministry." Appointments to the group would be in the hands of a group

of presidents of universities. Such a group would be a private

censorship board.

A different form of private censorship was suggested by the Boston

director of the local Legion of Decency movement in that area. His

plan called for a private censor at the regional exchange center of

distribution, with the power to prohibit the exhibition of objectionable

---

1. Statement issued by the Episcopal Committee, February 25, 1936.
2. Ibid.
3. The New York times, July 16, 1934, July 17, 1934.
4. Goldstein, in Perlman, op. cit., pp. 227 f.

pictures and scenes.

The Episcopal Committee chose not to direct the Legion's pressure toward such forms of private censorship. It made no public or private statement, so far as is known, which would indicate the norms which governed this choice.

"Reform by kindness".--Thorp has used the expression "reform by kindness," to describe the policy of those groups who had previously espoused the "praise the best, ignore the rest" strategy.[1] The Episcopal Committee, by proposing the sanction of the buyers' strike, rejected this policy. Technical norms of efficiency dictated that this policy, ineffective for so many years, be dropped.

Effective self-regulation.--The policy actually adopted by the Committee was that of directing the Legion's social pressure toward making efficient the system of self-control already existing in the Hays office regulation of film content in accordance with the provisions of the Production Code.

Two months after the announcement of the Legion of Decency campaign, the Motion Picture Producers and Distributors of America, Inc., met in New York. At this meeting it was decided to make radical changes in the organization of the machinery for enforcing the Production Code. It was agreed that submission of scripts before the start of production be made mandatory. The jury of producers was eliminated as a court of appeal. The sole and final decision on appeal from judgments of the Production Code Administration was lodged with the Board of Directors of the M.P.P.D.A., in New York. The trade

1. Thorp, op. cit., p. 167.

association agreed that no member would exhibit in its theaters any picture which did not bear the seal of approval of the P.C.A.

A week later the Episcopal Committee, meeting at Archbishop McNicholas' residence in Cincinnati, was informed of these changes. It was also told that Joseph I. Breen, who had been in charge of the Production Code Administration since the preceding December, would be given much more local authority, and that the P.C.A. personnel would be increased to a sufficient number to adequately handle its work.

Up to this point, the Episcopal Committee had not committed the Legion to any objective more definite than "reform" by the industry. After prolonged discussion at this meeting, the Committee decided that if the industry actually made the proposed changes, and abided by them, the objectives of the campaign would be achieved. In a statement to the press it said:

> The Episcopal Committee views with favor the renewed efforts of the organized industry to discharge its responsibility of issuing only such motion pictures as may conform with reasonable moral standards. The Committee believes that the Production Code if given adequate enforcement will materially and constructively influence the character of screen entertainment. Hence it is disposed to lend encouragement and cooperation to these efforts which it hopes will achieve the desired results.[1]

The result of this conference between the Committee and the representatives of the film industry was to commit the campaign, as far as the Episcopal Committee could do so, to the policy of directing the Legion's pressure toward effective self-regulation by the industry of motion picture content. With this statement, the Committee linked the

---

1. "Report, p. 27.

campaign to the earlier effort to create pressure for enforcement of the Production Code.

It was clear from the statement that the Committee had not brought the campaign to an end. Its approval of the reorganization of the Production Code Administration was tentative. What the Committee had done was to establish the relative positions of the Hays office and the Legion of Decency. Authoritative control was left in the hands of the Hays office; the Legion was dedicated to the maintenance of pressure to ensure that the Hays office exercised that control effectively.

The norms which dictated this choice were partly ethical, inasmuch as it involved approbation for the standards of the Production Code, and partly efficiency norms, inasmuch as it involved the judgment that the reorganized Production Code Administration could effectively control the morals of the movies. The norms which governed the choice of self-regulation by the industry will be clarified in the concluding chapter.[1]

Local Bishops

The principal function of the Bishops in their local dioceses was that of recruiting the following of the Legion of Decency. A minor function was the exercise of pressure on their own account upon the exhibitors of movies in their own dioceses.

The recruiting function was carried out through the process of communicating to the potential followers the elements of the process of social action which the Bishops wished to inaugurate. The

---

1. Infra, pp. 192-194.

communication pattern itself has been outlined in the analysis of the
structure of the Legion.[1] The ends of the action process, as proposed
by the Bishops, were indicated in the previous chapter on values. The
means proposed by the Bishops, the buyers' strike, will be more
appropriately treated in the next section. The element to be
considered here is the normative guidance which the Bishops proposed
to their followers.

The norms proposed by the Bishops to guide the followers towards
choice of the buyers' strike as a means of putting pressure on the
movie industry are implied in the pledge which the Bishops circulated, and stated explicitly in their communications to their followers.

The pledge.--The first pledge formula, "used in almost all
dioceses in its original form," was issued in April, 1934. It read:

> I wish to join the Legion of Decency, which condemns
> vile and unwholesome moving pictures. I unite with all who
> protest against them as a grave menace to youth, to home
> life, to country and to religion.
> I condemn absolutely those salacious motion pictures
> which, with other degrading agencies, are corrupting
> public morals and promoting a sex mania in our land.
> I shall do all that I can to arouse public opinion
> against the portrayal of vice as a normal condition of
> affairs, and against depicting criminals of any class
> as heroes and heroines, presenting their filthy philo-
> sophy of life as something acceptable to decent men and
> women.
> I unite with all who condemn the display of suggestive
> advertisements on bill-boards, at theatre entrances and
> the favorable notices given to immoral motion pictures.
> Considering these evils, I hereby promise to remain
> away from all motion pictures except those which do not
> offend decency and Christian morality. I promise further
> to secure as many members as possible for the Legion of
> Decency.
> I make this protest in a spirit of self-respect and
> with the conviction that the American public does not
> demand filthy pictures, but clean entertainment and
> educational features.[2]

1. Supra, pp. 54 f.
2. "Report," p. 4.

This lengthy pledge puts most of its emphasis upon the character
of the object towards which hostility was to be aroused. A later
form of the pledge, adopted at the November, 1934, meeting of the
National Catholic Welfare Conference, takes the values more for granted,
and emphasizes instead the overt action pledged and the norms guiding
that choice. This form is much shorter; it is the form used up to
the present in the annual oral renewal of the pledge in all Catholic
churches.

> I condemn indecent and immoral pictures, and those
> which glorify crime or criminals.
> I promise to do all that I can to strengthen
> public opinion against the production of indecent and
> immoral films, and to unite with all who protest them.
> I acknowledge my obligation to form a right
> conscience about pictures that are dangerous to my
> moral life. As a member of the Legion of Decency, I
> pledge myself to remain away from them. I promise,
> further, to stay away altogether from places of
> amusement which show them as a matter of policy.[1]

The norms implied in this pledge are, first, the obligation as
a socius, a member of human society, to show regard for the welfare
of fellow members, and, second, the individual's obligation to
preserve his own moral integrity.

Communications from the Bishops.--These norms were stated
explicitly in the Bishops' appeals for followers. The Bishops urged
their people to refuse patronage to objectionable movies, i.e., to
adopt the means proposed by the Legion of Decency, on the grounds that
such action was dictated by the twofold obligation as a socius and as
an individual. Several examples of each are quoted from the "Report":

(1) The obligation as socius:

> This particular obligation is overlooked by the indi-
> vidual who thinks only of the probability of evil to which

---

1. "Report", p. 379.

he himself is exposed and ignores the probability
of evil to which a whole class of spectators may
be exposed, resulting in the weakening of their
moral stamina and the undermining of the good of
society at large. Hence it is that the conscience
of the individual is burdened not only with the
care of himself but with the care of his neighbor....[1]
        Christ's law of loving our neighbor constrains us
to action;...[2]
        A serious lowering of the moral standards of any
community menaces the common good and weakens, if it
does not destroy, the sanctions that guarantee peace
and prosperity.... Evil motion pictures in their
baneful influence undermine the moral foundations of
the state.[3]
        Every Catholic...must look to the common good
and avoid what causes injury to the souls of others.
When he patronizes motion pictures of a vile
character he is culpable...because he supports a
form of amusement that spreads moral contagion in
the community.[4]
        Happily American Catholics nowadays seem to
realize that they have a responsibility to the
society in which they live, especially to the
children,...[5]
        Parents cannot ignore their serious obligation
to safeguard their children.[6]
        We shall no longer be placed in the silly and
shameful position of financing our own degradation
and the ruin of our children.[7]

(2) The obligation as an individual:

        The individual conscience must be rightly formed
and must in the court of God oblige one to avoid what
is morally wrong and morally dangerous.[8]
        And now, what does the Legion of Decency ask of
you? Its request is a simple one. It asks that you
individually remain away from the presentation of
films which offend the moral law and the precepts of
decency.[9]
        Everyone is bound in conscience, under pain of sin,
to refrain from attending the exhibition of any harmful

---

1. Archbishop Murray, "Report," p. 85.
2. Bishop Gallagher, ibid., p. 108.
3. Cardinal Hayes, ibid., p. 19.
4. Bishop McDevitt, ibid., p. 150.
5. Bishop Armstrong, ibid., p. 91.
6. Archbishop McNicholas, ibid., p. 80.
7. Cardinal O'Connell, ibid., pp. 7 f.
8. Archbishop McNicholas, ibid., p. 53.
9. Bishop Kelly, ibid., p. 135.

or immoral picture.[1]
    Catholics must not go into the occasions of sin,
they must not expose themselves to any experience
that almost invariably leads them from the path of
virtue.[2]

No other constraints than those deriving from the twofold

obligation of these norms were imposed by the Bishops. The Bishops

issued no commands in virtue of their spiritual authority. "The

Catholic Bishops have as yet," said Archbishop McNicholas in September,

1934, "exercised no compulsion in calling attention of their people

to the menace of the indecent moving picture."[3]

    The pledge itself was not construed by the Bishops as imposing

any new constraint. This was clearly indicated in many of the

Bishops' statements, e.g.:

    Everything contained in the pledge is a duty of
conscience independently of the pledge and independently of membership in the Legion of Decency.[4]
    The Legion simply emphasizes an obligation
already binding upon you and strengthens what God
has already required.[5]
    In the matter of the obligatory force of the
pledge it may be stated in the instruction and to
those who make inquiries, that it...does not in
itself bind in conscience.[6]

Direct pressure from Bishops.--A secondary function exercised

by many local Bishops was that of exerting pressure directly upon

the local exhibitors of movies. The pattern of this activity was

furnished by a letter written in February, 1934, by the Bishop of

---

1. Bishop Conroy, "Report," p. 102.
2. Bishop McDevitt, ibid., p. 150.
3. Radio address, Blue Network, September 21, 1934, "Report," p. 53.
4. Archbishop Murray, "Report," p. 86.
5. Bishop Kelly, ibid., p. 135.
6. Archbishop Beckman, ibid., p. 73.

Monterey-Fresno to the manager of a theater in his diocese:

> This letter is to inform you that we are undertaking a
> campaign against indecent shows, which are corrupting par-
> ticularly the youth of our country.
> As you know the Catholic Church has continually been on
> the liberal side of the amusement question. We have not
> opposed, for example, baseball or theatrical amusements on
> Sunday. We are not supporters of so-called blue-laws. We
> encourage clean wholesome recreation at all times for our
> people and shall continue to do so.
> In waging this campaign against indecent shows we want
> you, as manager of a local theater, to know that the campaign
> is not against you. We know that many managers of our
> theaters are just as anxious as any of us to eliminate
> indecent shows, but that your hands have been tied by blind
> booking and other practices on the part of film producers....
> We would very much appreciate your bringing this campaign
> to the attention of film producers. You may assure them that
> it is not our wish to injure their business. But we do
> insist on decent shows, and intend to unite with other
> organizations and do everything in our power to compel
> elimination of filth, and thus safeguard the youth of our
> country from corruption.[1]

This letter was made the basis of a draft letter which was sent to
all the Bishops by Bishop Cantwell of the Episcopal Committee, with the
request that they send a similar letter to all theater managers in
their respective dioceses. According to the "Report," many Bishops
complied with this request.[2]

The Following

The function of the followers was to exert pressure upon the motion
picture industry by withdrawing its patronage from objectionable pictures.

Type of pressure.--The sanction of withdrawing patronage was
usually termed a "boycott." A boycott is a collective withdrawal

---

1. "Report," pp. 262 f. This activity seems to have given rise to a false
report that priests had been asked to inquire into minute details of
the financial conditions of all local theaters. Such a report originally appeared in Variety, April 10, 1934; it was repeated by the
Literary digest, May 5, 1934, and by Christian century, May 16, 1934.
Janes has quoted it, op. cit., p. 48.
2. Ibid., p. 257.

from economic or social relations with offending groups or individuals.[1]
When employers refuse to hire certain men, the boycott is called a
"blacklist"; when employees refuse to work, it is called a "strike."
The strike and the blacklist are specific forms of boycott. In economic
relations, when the term is used without modifiers, it signifies a
withdrawal of patronage, a refusal to buy from offending sellers.

The end of consumers' boycotts may be a reduction in price,
improvement in the quality of the goods, or in the labor conditions
under which the goods are produced, or punishment of the seller for
some political or social offense.[2]

The function of such boycotts is the restriction of the market
to the extent that profits are diminished.

There exists a legal classification of boycotts into primary
and secondary. The basis of the distinction is not always the same;
most often it seems to depend upon whether the boycott is carried out
by the offended parties alone, or whether they try to induce third
parties to refuse patronage.[3]

In the case of the Legion of Decency, the generic term "boycott"
is undoubtedly applicable to the withdrawal of patronage agreed upon
by the followers.

The use of this sanction assumed two forms, however, in the
Legion campaign. The first and almost universal one was the withdrawal
from only those pictures which were considered objectionable. The
second, used only in Philadelphia and perhaps in some isolated small

1. Harry W. Laidler, "Boycott," Encyclopedia of the social sciences, II,
   p. 662. Cf. Bernard, Social control, pp. 390-395; Ross, Social
   control, p. 92.
2. Ibid., p. 663.
3. Ibid., p. 665.

areas elsewhere, consisted in the withdrawal of patronage from all motion pictures.

Because the terms "primary boycott" and "secondary boycott" are already in use, it seems best to the author to reserve the unmodified term "boycott" for the second form, wherein all movies were included in the withdrawal. For the first form, the term "buyers' strike" is appropriate.[1]

Bernard instances as a case of "buyers' strike" the action of some housewives who collectively refused to buy meat because its price was too high.[2] He indicates no basis for distinguishing the buyers' strike from the boycott. His case is an instance of a selective refusal to buy a single article, rather than an unselective refusal to buy anything sold by an offending seller. Most boycotts are refusal to buy anything made by an offending producer, or sold by an offending dealer; they are unselective. The buyers' strike is a selective boycott.

The buyers' strike was the mode of action followed in all dioceses except Philadelphia. Most, as has been noted, used the pledge as originally formulated. In this pledge the promise was made "to remain away from all motion pictures except those which do not offend decency and Christian morality." The shorter form of the pledge contained the promise to refuse patronage to "pictures that are dangerous to my moral life."

In the shorter pledge, too, the stricter sanction of boycott

---

1. This term was used to describe the Legion activity in "Topics of the times," The New York times, July 14, 1934: "But it is hard to see how censorship figures in what is essentially a buyers' strike."
2. Bernard, op. cit., p. 386.

was directed toward those theaters which show "such pictures as a matter of policy."

The one large diocese to use the strong sanction of boycotting all motion picture theaters was Philadelphia. Cardinal Dougherty wrote in a pastoral letter:

> Nothing is left for us except the boycott, and this we must put in force if we are to achieve success. The Catholic people of this diocese are, therefore, urged to register their united protest against immoral and indecent films by remaining away entirely from all motion picture theaters.[1]

Locally, this action seems to have resulted in severe economic losses to exhibitors. Within a month, the manager of the Warner chain which controlled exhibition in Philadelphia, threatened to close his theaters.[2]

Nationally, the Philadelphia action brought the Legion to the attention of the country as a whole. It received wide publicity. The Times issue of June 9, which reported the Cardinal's letter, mentioned the Legion of Decency for the first time; thereafter there were reports on the Legion almost every day.

Other dioceses did not follow the example of Philadelphia, however. At the November meeting of the Bishops in 1934 a proposal that the boycott sanction be used by other dioceses was vetoed.[3]

Intensity of the pressure.--One of the most satisfactory measures of the intensity of the pressure created by the Legion of Decency would be figures indicating the decline in box-office receipts attributable to the Legion's withdrawal of patronage. Unfortunately there is no such

1. Cardinal Dougherty, May 23, 1934, "Report,", pp. 10f.
2. The New York times, July 4, 1934, July 8, 1934.
3. "Report," pp. 382 f.

evidence.

Such statements as were made during the campaign were not
consistent. Thus, Variety reported in July little or no marked
effect on the box offices from the movement.[1] Shortly after, The
Billboard reported that in the East the campaign had caused a falling
off of twenty per cent in the smaller cities.[2] In August, the New
York Daily News reported that attendance figures, "since the July
heat wave," were "substantially higher" than at the same time last
year.[3] The next day, the Wall Street Journal reported "the usual
summer slump," but added that figures were "slightly ahead" of the
same time the year before.[4] Less than two weeks after this, Standard
Statistics Company published an analysis of the film industry which
said, "Continued Church opposition to the motion picture industry
threatens to prevent the full fall seasonal recovery in box-office
sales."[5]

The fact is that there were no over-all statistics on box office
receipts. Such data as could be given on a local basis was concealed
as a trade secret.[6]

Janes' study was an attempt to measure the intensity of the Legion's
pressure in the Chicago area by comparing the showings of "condemned"
pictures in "high-Catholic" and "low-Catholic" districts for the
period April-May, 1934, and for the period September-October, 1934.[7]

---

1. Quoted in The New York times, July 11, 1934.
2. Quoted in The Catholic news, New York, August 4, 1934.
3. New York Daily news, August 31, 1934.
4. Wall Street journal, August 22, 1934.
5. Quoted in Los Angeles times, September 2, 1934.
6. Janes, op. cit., pp. 7 f.
7. Ibid., p. 3. Janes uses the term "high-Catholic" to describe districts
   having a Catholic population higher than the 23.6 per cent average for
   the whole city; "low-Catholic" districts are those with less than this
   average.

He found that seven of seventeen houses in low-Catholic districts,
and fourteen of sixteen houses in high-Catholic districts showed fewer
"condemned" films after the advent of the Legion than before.[1]

The best indication of the intensity of the pressure of the Legion
is given, not by figures, but by the reaction of the film industry to
the pressure.

Social pressure is effective only insofar as it is felt by those
against whom it is directed. In this case, it was the movie industry's
definition of the situation which mattered. The industry clearly
felt itself to be the object of very intense pressure. For the
industry took quick and firm steps in the direction of changing the
product which it had been told was unsatisfactory.

The offer to strengthen the Production Code enforcement procedure
was the first sign that the industry felt the pressure.

More important, there was a change in the content of the motion
picture product, dating from the reorganization of the Production
Code Administration.

Evidence of the change is found in the ratings of the very
critical Chicago Council of the Legion of Decency. Early in July,
before there were any pictures produced under the new regime, this
group published a list of feature pictures then current. It judged
thirty of the one hundred and twenty-five pictures listed to be
"immoral and unfit." Of the pictures released between July 15 and
the end of the year, however, only four were so condemned by the
Chicago group.

----

1. Janes, op. cit., p. 3.

Professional critics reported the change. By mid-December, a critic in The New York Times reported:

> Since Joseph Breen's board of control began to operate
> last summer there has been an obvious improvement in
> themes and a noticeable diminution in the kind of
> appalling cheapness and unintelligence which filmgoers
> deplore without regard to private allegiances of faith
> or creed.[1]

Shortly afterwards, a report from Hollywood said:

> Better pictures, morally and artistically have been
> made since regulation began than in many years
> before.... The cinema has learned, somewhat against
> its will, that purity pays.[2]

Means Used in the Permanent Process

The process of formation came to an end when the Bishops formally resolved, November, 1934, that the Legion of Decency should be a permanent institution.

The principal addition, during this period, to the means-pattern used by the Legion has been the reviewing and rating activity.

Two questions arise from the consideration of the reviewing and rating activity as a means used by the Legion. First, what is the precise function of this activity? Is it censorship? Second, what sort of constraint do the ratings impose upon Legion followers? Is it obedience to authority?

Rating and Censorship

Popularly, any process which results in the restriction of public expression of any sort is taken to be censorship. The Legion is often

1. The New York times, December 16, 1934.
2. Douglas W. Churchill, "Hollywood discovers that virtue pays," The New York times magazine, January 20, 1935.

called a censoring agency. Thus, in 1938, the Executive Secretary of the Legion was invited to uphold the affirmative in a radio debate on the subject: "Should motion pictures be censored?"[1]

The Legion, on the other hand, insists that it does not "censor" pictures. Very recently, the Executive Secretary reiterated this stand: "...it is important to note that the Legion of Decency is not a censorship body. Censorship implies statutory authorization, police power and absolute pre-release control of films."[2]

Some sociologists use the concept of censorship in such a way as to imply that they go no further than the popular acceptation. Looking at it from the point of view of the public, Lumley speaks of it as a barrier between the public and the event; a limitation of access to the real environment.[3] Landis, similarly, includes in the concept any limitation of messages transmitted over agencies of mass impression.[4] Both authors are discussing the concept in connection with propaganda. Taking the viewpoint of the one who communicates, Ross includes in the concept any hindrance of access of the artist to the public, whether by officials, or by critics, publishers, churches or other organized and unorganized groups.[5]

One is at liberty to define censorship, as any other concept, as he pleases. But for scientific purposes it is more fruitful to define concepts rigorously so that significant differences may be more clearly manifested.

---

1. Letter, Theodore Irwin, American Civil Liberties Union, to Rev. John J. McClafferty, June 2, 1938.
2. Letter, America, LXXII (February 3, 1945), 359.
3. Lumley, Means of social control, pp. 203 f.
4. Landis, Social control, pp. 199 f.
5. Ross, Social control, pp. 272 ff.

More acceptable, from this point of view, is the concept proposed
by Bernard, which limits its extension to that rejection of ideas and
data which is exercised by a body or organization endowed with power.[1]
Lasswell goes a step further and limits the notion of power to that
power which is also authoritative.

> Censorship is the policy of restricting public expression
> of ideas, opinions, conceptions and impulses which have or
> are believed to have the capacity to undermine the governing
> authority or the social and moral order which that authority
> considers itself bound to protect.[2]

The concept thus defined has two essential elements. One is negative, the restriction imposed upon communication. The other is positive,
the restriction comes from an agent endowed with authoritative power.[3]

The fruitfulness of using the more rigorously defined concept does
not consist in the fact that it exempts the Legion from the opprobrium
which is contemporarily connected with the term "censor." Its utility
lies in the fact that it enables one to understand the difference between
the Hays office influence on movie production and that of the Legion. It
thus makes it possible to understand the character of the total control
process.

The distinction was offered in the first chapter between authoritative controls and social pressures.[4] Pressure is that species of
control which operates without direct, authoritarian power. The Hays
office has such direct, authoritarian power over the content of films;
it is the control group. The Legion of Decency does not exercise that

1. Bernard, op. cit., p. 321.
2. Harold D. Lasswell, "Censorship," Encyclopedia of the social sciences,
   III, p. 290.
3. Modern totalitarian societies have introduced positive interference,
   imposing definite trends on cultural activity, attempting to shape
   the mentality of the people. Cf. Timasheff, "The legal regimentation
   of culture in National Socialist Germany," Fordham law review, XI
   (1942), 1-29, and "Cultural order in liberal, fascist and communist
   society," The American Catholic sociological review, III (1942), 63-71.
4. Supra, pp. 29 f.

kind of power; it is a pressure group.

When the Bishops met, in November, 1934, several proposals relative to the rating activity were presented. Among them was the suggestion that "one well-trained censor" should work in close collaboration with the industry's Production Code Administration. This would have given the Legion's representative some share in the authoritative control exercised through the Production Code Administration.

The proposal was vetoed. Archbishop Mooney, chairman of the Administrative Board of the National Catholic Welfare Conference, said, "We desire effective guidance, rather than efficient censorship."[1]

Not quite two years later, Archbishop McNicholas answered a public criticism made by G. B. Shaw:

> The Legion of Decency has no connection directly or indirectly with the Hays organization.... The Legion of Decency has no part in this self-regulatory body nor has it any responsibility for it.[2]

Will Hays has said the same thing: "the Legion of Decency does not censor motion pictures and has no authority to remove footage from American films."[3]

The most evident confirmation of this fact is the condemnation of "C" pictures by the Legion, and the number of pictures produced by members of the Hays organization which the Legion has rated "B". If the Legion had direct, authoritative control over film production, such pictures would not have been released.

---

1. "Report," p. 381.
2. Motion picture daily, September 16, 1936.
3. Quoted in "Report to the Episcopal Committee," 1943.

What, then, is the function of the Legion rating activity? It is
to provide the "effective guidance" mentioned by Archbishop Mooney.
The Bishops, during the Legion campaign, had urged upon their followers
the avoidance of "occasions of sin." This normative guidance needed
implementation. The ratings provide it, by telling which films are
more or less apt to be such "occasions." In other words, the lists
make concrete the abstract course of action considered desirable in
the norm.[1]

In the total control pattern, then, the Hays office is the only
source of direct, authoritative control. The Legion is a pressure
group, aimed originally at imposing, and since then at maintaining
a high level of effectiveness in the operation of the industry's process
of self-regulation. The rating activity is an implementation of the
norms proposed to the followers for their guidance in selecting as a
sanction the withdrawal of patronage from objectionable pictures. The
operation of this sanction is designed to make unprofitable the
production of objectionable pictures.

If the Bishops and their auxiliaries, the reviewers, are substituted
for the "ten thousand influential," the process of Legion pressure
bears a striking likeness to a proposal made by Ross over thirty years
before the emergence of the Legion.

> It may be that the fate of the artists' work should
> be decided by the ten thousand influential, subject to
> an appeal to the million uninfluential; the latter to
> ban without ruth or scruple whatever gives moral
> offense. In this way it may be possible to make art
> amenable to society without making it amenable to law.[2]

1. Cf. Parsons, op. cit., p. 75.
2. Ross, op. cit., p. 274.

Ratings and Obedience

What is the character of the constraint upon its followers imposed
by the ratings of the Legion? Are these implementations of the general
norms mandatory upon the followers? Putting the question another way,
are the ratings ethical or legal norms?

If the ratings partake of the character of legal norms, the
obligation to avoid condemned pictures would be one of obedience.

This is the case with the well known Index of Prohibited Books.[1]
Books listed by name in this list are forbidden to Catholics by those
with spiritual authority over them.

Such is not the case with the Legion's ratings.

> The approval of the Commission of Selection by
> the Bishops, it would seem, does not impose in
> itself upon the faithful a duty of obedience with
> regard to the judgments issued by the Commission....
> The importance and value of the moral ratings of
> films, stemming from the significance of the work
> and the competence of the reviewers, corroborated by
> the official character of the reviewing and rating
> body create for the faithful an obligation of prudence
> to take into consideration such ratings.[2]

The constraint imposed by the ratings, then, is one of prudence,
not one of obedience. The normative guidance is ethical, not legal
in character.

The difference between the Index and the Legion ratings can best
be understood within the framework of the Catholic understanding of
law, natural and human.[3]

1. Cf. George Haven Putnam, The censorship of the Roman Catholic Church,
2 vols., N.Y., G. P. Putnam's Sons, 1906-1907; Joseph M. Pernicone,
The ecclesiastical prohibition of books, Catholic University of
America Studies in Canon Law, Washington, D.C., Catholic University
of America, 1932.
2. "Considerations of the problem of the obligations arising from the
classifications made and issued by the Legion of Decency," (mimeographed), n.d., p. 4.
3. St. Thomas Aquinas, Summa theologica, 1-2, qq. 90-97.

The fundamental consideration is that what ought-to-be is determined by the ultimate end or purpose of man's actions. The Creator
of men wills that men do what ought-to-be done so that they will
achieve the end for which He created them. Man, accordingly, is so
constituted that he recognizes an innate imperative to do what ought-
to-be done. This imperative, in conjunction with the reasoning power
which enables man to discover what ought-to-be done, is the "natural law."

The imperatives of the natural law are general; there is often
need to particularize them to fit particular situations, particular
institutions. Because man is a social being, someone has to have
authority to make these particularizations.[1] When particularizations
of the natural law are made by human authority, they constitute human
law.

Ecclesiastical law is of this latter category.

In the case of books, the Catholic understanding is that natural
law forbids the reading of such books as are likely to jeopardize the
attainment of man's end. Ecclesiastical law has particularized the
natural law to the extent of imposing a mandate which forbids reading
of whole classes of books, such as those which tend to undermine the
foundations of religion, or are professedly obscene.[2] In the Index,
the Church goes a step further and announces that the books listed there
are definitely in the forbidden categories.

In the case of the movies, the Catholic understanding is that
natural law forbids attendance at such movies as are likely to jeopardize
the attainment of man's end, just as in the case of books. But

1. St. Thomas Aquinas, De regimine principum, I, 1.
2. Pernicone, op. cit., pp. 123-187.

ecclesiastical authority has not particularized the natural law to
the extent of forbidding certain categories of movies, nor of
listing single pictures which are definitely within the scope of
natural law.

In the case of prohibited books, the Church implements the norms
of natural law by imposing an authoritative prohibition against
reading particular books. In the case of the movies, the Church
implements norms of natural law by offering a prudential guide for
the selection of film entertainment which will not violate the norms
of what ought-to-be seen.

Effectiveness of the Permanent Process

The primary, minimum criterion of the effectiveness of Legion
pressure during the ten years of its permanent existence is the
incidence of "condemned" films on the entertainment market. The
secondary criterion is the incidence of "B" films, "objectionable in
part."

The effectiveness of the Legion, as far as condemned pictures are
concerned, is evidenced by the practically complete absence of major
condemned films from the market since February, 1936. Seven major
productions were condemned by the Legion in this period. Six of these
were revised, either before release, or soon after. The other, which
has not received the Hays office seal, has not been given general
exhibition.

The rest of the condemned list is composed of foreign productions,
or domestic "quickies" which have a most limited circulation. In the
total picture, they are unimportant details.

With regard to "B" pictures, the situation is not quite as clear.

First of all, the "B" category is not as clearly defined as is the "C". From the beginning it has been a residual classification. Pictures which did not certainly belong in either the "condemned" or the "unobjectionable" categories were placed in this in-between class.

The succession of captions used in the first two years of listing activity are indicative of this fact.

The original caption used in the Chicago list read:

> (1) Pictures in this group are considered more or less objectionable in spots because of their possible suggestiveness or vulgarity or sophistication or lack of modesty. Neither approved nor forbidden, but for adults only.

This caption was succeeded by a series of emendations which eliminated the expression "forbidden," eliminated the reasons for the rating because they were not strictly "moral" considerations, and alternately eliminated and restored the reference to adults. Successively the following captions were used:

> Accepted with reservation.

> Not recommended. Pictures in this classification are neither recommended nor are they condemned because partly unsatisfactory either in subject matter or treatment.

> Not recommended. Pictures in this classification are adjudged to be unsatisfactory in part either because of the subject matter or treatment.

> Disapproved for youth with a word of caution even for adults.

> Objectionable in part.[1]

Secondly, the constraint upon followers to refuse patronage to

---

1. The caption, "objectionable in part," has been used without change since early in 1936.

"B" pictures is not as clearly defined, nor as strong as is that
related to "C" films. This fact is indicated by the successive use in
the above captions of the expressions, "accepted," "not recommended,"
"disapproved," and "objectionable."

The Legion urges its followers to stay away from "B" films, but
it has not issued any definitive statement as to the character and
extent of the obligation to do so.

Because the "B" classification is a residual category, it
contains films whose violation of the accepted standards may be very
slight, or more serious up to the point where they are just short of
being condemned. The effectiveness of the Legion with regard to "B"
films, consequently, cannot be adequately measured by the incidence
of "B" pictures on the market.

And because the obligation to avoid "B" pictures is not as strong
or as clear as that to avoid "C" pictures, the full force of Legion
pressure is not exercised in the case of "B" films. Consequently,
their presence on the market is not a complete test of Legion effectiveness.

With these reservations in mind, it is, nevertheless,
instructive to examine the number of "B" pictures in proportion to
the total number of films reviewed.

Table 5 shows that the proportion of "B" pictures produced by
the eight leading producers in the United States has ranged, between
February, 1936 and November, 1944, from six to fifteen per cent of the
total output. The average for the whole period is less than ten per
cent.

It is difficult to discover any trend from these figures. Table 6 shows a comparison of the last year's ratings with those of the previous years. Numerically, the proportion of "B" pictures in the past year's list is higher than that for the previous period. And while it is lower than for the preceding year, the last half of the period, beginning in November, 1940, shows a twelve per cent proportion of "B" pictures, as compared with seven and one-half per cent for the first half of the period.

TABLE 5

PICTURES PRODUCED BY EIGHT MAJOR COMPANIES RATED "B"
BY THE LEGION OF DECENCY, FEBRUARY, 1936
TO NOVEMBER, 1944, BY YEARS

Year	Pictures Produced	"B" Pictures	Per cent "B" Pictures
1936-37	662	53	8.1
1937-38	340	20	5.9
1938-39	391	23	5.9
1939-40	372	36	9.7
1940-41	365	42	11.5
1941-42	376	36	9.6
1942-43	281	41	14.6
1943-44	272	35	12.9
Total	3059	286	9.3

Source: Legion of Decency Films Reviewed.

It is impossible to discover whether the increase in the proportion of "B" pictures in recent years reflects a drop in the intensity of Legion pressure, or a relaxation in the efficiency of the Production Code Administration, or a change toward greater severity in the judgments of the Legion reviewers.

TABLE 6

PICTURES PRODUCED BY EIGHT MAJOR COMPANIES RATED "B"
BY THE LEGION OF DECENCY, FEBRUARY, 1936 TO
NOVEMBER, 1943, AND NOVEMBER, 1943 TO
NOVEMBER, 1944, BY COMPANIES

Company	1936-1943			1943-1944		
	Total	"B"	%	Total	"B"	%
Columbia	423	30	7.1	49	5	10.2
M-G-M	374	36	9.6	29	3	10.3
Paramount	382	40	10.5	31	10	32.3
R.K.O.	356	26	7.6	37	3	8.1
Twentieth Century-Fox	415	28	6.7	30	2	6.6
United Artists	162	29	18.0	19	3	15.8
Universal	357	27	7.6	55	4	7.3
Warner	318	35	11.0	22	5	22.7
Total	2787	251	9.0	272	35	12.9

Source: Legion of Decency Films Reviewed.

Conclusion

The foregoing study of the means used by the Legion of Decency
to impose and maintain motion picture conformity with the ideal
patterns embodied in the standards of the Production Code would seem
to justify the following empiric generalization.

A given code of standards and regulations may be accepted as
embodying either technical or ethical rules.

If it is accepted as an ethical code, violations may be due to
ignorance or to a conflict of interests. Such violations may be
judged and penalized by a jury of peers which accepts the code as
ethical.

If the code is accepted as a technical code only, its constraining

power is derived only from the will to act efficiently or expediently.
In the case of one who produces for profits, economic success is the
value which supplies the constraining-force. When such a producer violates
the rules, he can be brought back to conformity either by force or by
restoring the conditions which make the technical rules binding; that
is to say, conformity can be restored by law or by making it financially
unprofitable to produce in violation of the code.

In such a case the consumer is the only qualified judge. If he
is able, by concerted action, to make such production financially
unprofitable, he need not have recourse to the police power of the law.

If enough consumers are willing to accept the normative guidance
of a jury which rates the product's conformity with the code, their
free, collective withdrawal of patronage from the objectionable product
will bring the producer back to conformity with the code.

The Legion of Decency is an instance of the "triumph" of ethical
rules, imposed and enforced through purely ethical constraints.

CHAPTER V

THE LEGION OF DECENCY IN RELATION
TO OTHER GROUPS IN SOCIETY

In the preceding chapters, the Legion of Decency has been
subjected to a detailed analysis in which its structural and developmental processes have been viewed, as it were, from within. Only
obliquely has there been reference to the Legion's relations to other
groups in society. It would be a mistake to infer that the Legion's
activities have been carried on as though it were merely a matter
between itself and the motion picture industry. This chapter will
attempt to sketch in some of the details which fill out the picture.

One important feature must be omitted from this treatment. The
scope of this study excludes consideration of those cultural factors
which have conditioned the origin and development of the Legion. The
impact of the cultural environment upon the Legion is certainly a
relevant field of study for the complete understanding of the situation.[1] But an adequate consideration of the influence of this
factor must await a scientific study of the culture of the period;
none such exists thus far in sociological literature.

MacIver has said that "pressure groups, as distinct from class
groups, are characteristic of a heterogeneous and changing society."[2]
Whenever there is a pressure group, there is another group which does

1. Cf. Edwin M. Lemert, "The folkways and social control," American
   sociological review, VII (1942), 398.
2. MacIver, Encyclopedia of the social sciences, XII, p. 348.

not agree with it. Else there would be absolute unanimity, and no
need for pressure. Likewise, where there is pressure, changes are
being promoted or being resisted. That is what pressure is for. This
chapter will study the disagreement, alleged or real, with regard to
the changes being promoted or resisted by the Legion of Decency, as it
is manifested in other religious groups, the film critics, the "Left,"
the proponents and the opponents of governmental control. It will
conclude with a discussion of some implications of the autonomy of the
existing control system.

Other Religious Groups

The policy of the Legion of Decency is determined by the Roman
Catholic Bishops of the Episcopal Committee. Its local leaders are
Bishops. The reviewing body is exclusively Catholic. While the
followers include many who are not Catholics, it is undoubtedly
correct to refer to the Legion as a Catholic group.

Is this Catholic group, bringing pressure to bear on behalf of
its own moral standards, acting in opposition to other religious
groups with different standards? Is, therefore, the very existence
of the Legion an indication of heterogeneity and change in the moral
standards upheld by religious groups?

Minority Control

The Nation, lumping together those of other religious affiliations
and those of none under the inclusive term "non-Catholic," implies an
affirmative answer to the questions just raised:

> ...if one is a member of the Catholic church, one need
> not perhaps quarrel with...the ability of the church to
> recognize and protect Christian or "human" morality.

But some seventy millions of Americans attend the
movies every week, and in 1934 there were in the
United States something over twenty million Catholics.
What the non-Catholic movie goers are entitled to
decide, therefore, is whether they wish to have their
films censored in advance by the Catholic church.[1]

In similar vein, Thorp has written:

Though the Catholics are a minority group as compared
to Protestants and Jews, they are able by expert
organization to make their peculiar [sic] prejudices
prevail....It is the most deliberate attempt which has
yet been made to control the interests of the American
screen in the interest of a group.[2]

Rabbi Goldstein makes the same implication, saying, "No group,

whether it be selected by an official of the government or by a

Catholic, Protestant or Jewish body, has the right to make mandatory

upon the city or State or country standards that the group itself

believes at the time to be correct."[3]

Dr. Worth M. Tippy, Protestant churchman, expressed his private

view of the matter:

There are important differences in emphasis upon
moral and social issues between the Catholic church,
the Protestant and Jewish groups, and the general
public. It would be unfortunate if a strictly
Catholic point of view on particular controverted
issues were to determine decisions at Hollywood.[4]

The Protestant Digest, in a vigorous attack on the Legion, asserted,

"the minority control of the most vital amusement source of the nation

is one of the most astounding things in the history of the United States.[5]

1. "Vatican over Hollywood," The Nation, CXLII (July 11, 1936), 33; cf.
   "G.B.S. and the Catholic censorship," The new republic, LXXXVIII
   (September 22, 1936), 173.
2. Thorp, op. cit., pp. 208, 214.
3. Goldstein, op. cit., pp. 214 f.
4. Worth M. Tippy to Martin Quigley, March 20, 1935.
5. "Breen--super-censor," Protestant digest, June-July, 1940, quoted in
   "Report to the Episcopal Committee," 1940.

Homogeneous Values

The Legion has not answered such charges directly, but, in view of its repeated insistence upon the Ten Commandments, the "traditional," "truly American," "unchanging" "principles of morality," it is fair to assume that its answer would be somewhat as follows.

First, it does not follow from the fact that the Legion's personnel is predominantly Catholic that it is making "peculiar prejudices" prevail, nor that it is using its pressure to gain its own selfish interests. The issue is not strictly one of the religious affiliation of the group members and leaders; what is relevant is the character of the values it is supporting.

Second, there is a wide area of agreement on moral questions between the Catholic group and other religious groups. When the Catholic group acts in this field, it does not contradict the position of other religious groups.

Many statements have been made about the changing mores of American society. Tufts subtitled his book: "Dilemmas of the Changing Mores."[1] Waller's study of the contemporary American family offers a more detailed study of the conflict between ideal patterns and actual behavior patterns in those relationships which have been of much concern to the Legion of Decency.[2] But there has not been a corresponding effort put into the investigation of the extent to which the mores of contemporary society have remained constant and homogeneous.

In the case at hand, the observable fact is that such apprehensions

---

1. James H. Tufts, America's social morality, New York, Henry Holt and Company, 1933.
2. Willard Waller, The family: a dynamic interpretation, New York, The Dryden Press, 1939.

as Tippy's regarding "important differences" between the Catholic and other religious groups have not been borne out in the event. Tippy did not specify what these differences were; Goldstein, however, referred to divorce, birth control and suicide as important areas of disagreement.[1] Divorce and suicide have been the occasion of objection by the Legion without opposition from other religious groups. It has been pointed out previously that these issues have been met without incurring marked opposition from other religious groups. The fact of the matter is that while other religious groups may support a moral code which is not so steadfastly opposed to divorce and suicide as the Catholic code is, there is none whose code supports them as generally positive values. In the most important relationships of marriage, Tippy himself had noted that differences between the codes of religious groups pale before "their essential agreement on the sanctity and integrity of Christian marriage."[2] Since the Jewish code is notably insistent upon the same values, it can be included in the same category.

Evidence of this agreement is found in the lack of opposition to the Legion from religious sources. The author of the article in the Protestant Digest admitted "if any voice has been raised in protest, it has escaped the attention of this constant movie-goer."[3] Moreover, not only have other religious groups failed to oppose the Legion, they have largely ceased to sponsor or support such general attacks on movie morality as characterized the years before the Legion.

This silence in the presence of Legion activity may be interpreted,

1. Goldstein, op. cit., p. 215.
2. Tippy, loc. cit.
3. The Protestant Digest, loc. cit.

as the Protestant Digest article suggested, as the result of intimidation exercised by the Catholic church over the Press of the United
States. Or it may be due to apathy on the part of the other religious
group members. Or, on the other hand, it may be a sign of their tacit
consent and approval.

That the Catholic Church in the United States should be able to
intimidate the press to the extent that it would not report the dissatisfaction of other religious groups with the Legion of Decency would be
a most remarkable development in the religious history of this country.
But even in the unusual event that such intimidation should exist,
dissatisfaction among other religious groups would be expressed with
free rein in the pages of the numerous journals of Protestant and
Jewish groups. Thence it would surely find its way into the weekly
news magazines, and at least the correspondence columns of the daily
press. The rather complete absence of such items indicates that the
explanation by intimidation lacks foundation.

That other religious groups are apathetic toward the Legion's
standards and its pressure to maintain them seems highly improbable in
view of the past record of these groups in supporting pre-Legion attacks
on movie morals. With no evidence of such a radical change of
attitude, the explanation by apathy is unconvincing.

By process of elimination, then, that interpretation is most
probable which says that the Legion has been able to maintain its
pressure activities without notable opposition from other religious
groups because the bulk of the members of these groups support
essentially the same values as those upheld by the Legion of Decency.

This, it would seem, is partial evidence for the conclusion that in a large section of American society certain moral values are still homogeneous and constant.

It is not conclusive evidence. The possibility remains that support for these values is restricted to the ethical leaders of the other religious groups, that their followers do not recognize these values, yet are subject to compulsions not to vocalize their opposition. This, it may be submitted, seems unlikely in view of the tendency of the leaders of these groups to reflect rather than guide the attitudes of their followers, and in view of the positive support given the Legion by the members of these groups at the time of its formation in 1934.

There is, moreover, opposition from non-religious sources which probably reflects divergent attitudes toward moral standards. This is a boundary to the area of homogeneity and constancy. This opposition does not usually, however, vocalize its hostile attitude toward particular moral standards supported by the Legion; its opposition is usually predicated upon aesthetic or social considerations. The aesthetic values are the special concern of the professional film critics; these will be discussed next.

The Film Critics

Relations between the Legion and the professional film critics were not, at the beginning, cordial. The critics reacted negatively to the prospect of films' aesthetic values being strait-jacketed by a code of moral standards. They deplored, most of them, the artistically repulsive banality and salaciousness of the movies of the time, but they were inclined to the belief that these features were due in large measure

to the restrictions which prevented the films from outspoken defiance
of the traditional code of ethics. Only by casting off these
restrictions, they held, could the films make aesthetic advance.

This attitude long antedated the rise of the Legion. The Nation
had given consistent expression to it over the course of the previous
dozen years. The precise cast of this attitude, as well as its depth
and consistency, can best be seen from expressions of it. Those which
follow are all drawn from the pages of The Nation.

"Their tawdry, commercial, untruthful picture of life is the real
immorality."[1] Of a reforming official it was said that he "lets the
cat out of the bag when he denounces any play that 'contains words or
expressions doing violence to accepted standards.' Like all censors
he wants life petrified."[2] Art should not "pander to the traditional
in morality."[3] British film censorship is based upon "unrealistic
Sunday-school morality,...an elaborate code of social hypocrisy and
unreal convention."[4] The Hays office Production Code surrenders "every
right to sincerity," meantime respecting "all the prejudices of every
convention."[5] "By keeping the movies pure--that is, by forbidding any
frankly comic or frankly serious treatment of love in modern life--the
reformers have produced an endless crop of leering, hypocritical and
dishonest dramas."[6] Contemporary films, which are "the most completely
sex-soaked form of popular amusement ever provided to any society," are
that way because "whatever is straight, frank, honest and truth-telling"
has been ruled out of them."[7] "Hollywood has been forced into making

1. "Morals and the movies," The nation, CXII (April 20, 1921), 581.
2. "Film censors and other morons," ibid., CXVII (December 12, 1923),678.
3. Ibid., CXXIX (September 18, 1929), 291.
4. "British films are pure," ibid, CXXXI (November 19, 1930), 547.
5. "Virtue in cans," ibid., CXXX (April 16, 1930), 441.
6. "Celluloid sin," ibid., CXXXIV (June 29, 1932), 714.
7. "Celluloid czar," ibid., CXXXVII (July 11, 1934), 34.

an infantile salacity its stock in trade, largely because it is
forbidden to deal with nearly everything else."[1]

This attitude, with its jealous regard for aesthetic values, with
or without a denial of the value of the traditional standards, carried
over into the Legion campaign. Then the fear was expressed that the
Legion was going to sissify the movies, that it would insist upon the
production of only those pictures which could safely be presented to
children. The films of the morrow, it was said, would feature an
"All-Decent Life of Elsie Dinsmore, Played by Actors Who Say Their
Prayers Every Night and Never Chew Their Fingernails."[2] The rise of the
"cinema bootlegger" was predicted, and "movie speak-easies, to which we
shall furtively repair to see 'Little Man, What Now?' or 'Little Women'."[3]

There were, of course, subordinate and less idealistic reasons
for coolness toward the Legion campaign. Most of the critics are employed
by newspapers. The Philadelphia boycott produced a sharp drop in film
advertising in the daily press of that city. If the phenomenon spread,
there would be serious economic repercussions. Also, critics shared
the widespread apprehension of the press that a precedent was being set;
if the motion picture campaign succeeded, the press would be the next
to feel the pressure.[4]

In the event, time appears to have soothed the brow of the critics
who worried about the aesthetic future of the films. Pictures, they
saw, showed artistic improvement instead of the expected deterioration.

1. "The movie boycott," The nation, CXXXIX (July 11, 1934), 34.
2. Quoted in The Catholic news (New York), August 18, 1934.
3. Samuel Chotzinoff, "Words without music," New York post, July 9, 1934
4. Cf. Saturday review of literature, XXIII (December 22, 1934), 384.

Six months after the reorganization of the Production Code Administration
under Joseph I. Breen, a critic in The New York Times wrote:

> The Legion of Decency has exerted a profound
> influence upon the activities of the film city, and
> it has performed a service to film-goers everywhere
> by crippling the manufacture of such feeble-minded
> delicatessen as "All of Me," "Born to be Bad,"
> "Enlighten Thy Daughter," "The Life of Vergie
> Winters," "Limehouse Blues," and a number of other
> titles which will hurt nobody by their presence on
> the Legion's blacklist. Since Joseph Breen's board
> of control began to operate last Summer there has
> been an obvious improvement in themes and a
> noticeable diminution in the kind of appalling
> cheapness and unintelligence which filmgoers
> deplore without regard to private allegiance of
> faith or creed.[1]

From Hollywood, in January, 1935, came the report, "Better
pictures, morally and artistically have been made since regulation
began than in many years before."[2]

At this time, The Nation, while it conceded that the Legion's
activities were moderate "at least as far as reforming organizations
go," was still afraid. "We wonder, however, just how much of this
apparent moderation is due to the desire to enter a wedge,...to
grow less tolerant with the films as time goes on."[3]

But as time went on, the Legion incorporated into its classifications the distinction between films for adults and films for
children. Very few major productions produced in their entirety under
Breen's supervision were condemned. Meanwhile the pictures showed no
aesthetic depreciation which could be attributed to the moral
restrictions under which they were produced. At the end of ten years

1. The New York times, December 16, 1934.
2. Douglas W. Churchill, "Hollywood discovers that virtue pays," The
   New York times magazine, January 20, 1935.
3. "Black side of the white list," The nation, CXL (January 9, 1935),
   34.

of Legion activity, two nationally syndicated columnist critics

praised the Legion on the same day. The Legion, said one, "saved our

industry some years ago."[1] Another wrote,

> I am neither a Catholic nor an advocate for the
> censorship of motion pictures, but I doff my bonnet
> to the Legion of Decency and give it credit for a
> good job, well done. Not only has it imposed an
> effective check rein on salacious pictures, it has
> also done much to raise the artistic level of all
> films.[2]

A New York Times correspondent from Hollywood suggests how this

aesthetic advance has come to pass: "Hollywood is learning to use

finesse in dealing with a variety of plot situations which if treated

objectively [sic] or obviously, would be unsuitable."[3]

This does not mean that critics have gone over to the Legion camp

in a body. The legitimate conclusion is that the critics have had

little cause to object to the Legion on the grounds which provoked

their original hostility.

There have been adverse criticisms from critics in later years;

these have been directed mostly against the alleged influence of the

Legion on the movies' treatment of social questions. In this respect,

the hostile critics share the attitude common to those who are here

labelled "the left."

"The Left"

The unfortunate rubric which heads this division seems to be

the only one which would have a recognizable referent and at the same

---

1. Hedda Hopper, worcester daily telegram, December 2, 1944.
2. Jimmie Fidler, Worcester evening gazette, December 2, 1944.
3. Fred Stanley, The New York times, November 19, 1944.

time be broad enough to include the assorted sources from which has
sprung criticism of the Legion directed at its alleged efforts to
discourage the production of films dealing with criticism of the
existing social order. Classification of these diverse sources into
one category does not imply that they are at one in their positive
objectives; it is based on the fact that they are all critical of
society as it stands.

Criticism of this sort stems from political ideologists, churchmen,
film writers and producers, racial groups, and university professors.

At bottom, they all deplore the fact that contemporary movies are
made to entertain, rather than to inculcate certain social values.
"Our friends of the Left," a class at one university was told, "would
like to see the screen become a militant instrument in forging the
bonds of working class solidarity."[1]

Dr. Tippy presented the case against the Production Code in some
detail. This instrument, he held, is defective because it is

> too preoccupied with sex and...its moral concepts are
> too preponderantly individualistic. The Code does
> not take sufficient account of the moral standards
> which are emerging out of the present social ferment,
> and especially of the new concepts of industrial and
> political responsibility. The morality of collective
> action needs statement. The sin of war should be
> in the picture. The right of the cinema to portray
> vested evils and entrenched privileges in their true
> light, and to embody the struggle for social security
> and economic plenty...is a kind of morality concerning
> which the Code gives insufficient attention.[2]

Two years after this indictment, Dr. Tippy announced the organization
of "Associated Film Audiences," to stimulate the production of films

---

1. Howard S. Cullman, to Professor Frederick Thrasher's class in film
    appreciation, New York University, The New York times, January 8, 1937.
2. Worth M. Tippy to Martin Quigley, March 20, 1935.

"that give a true and socially useful portrayal of the contemporary scene."[1] Film Survey, the organ of this group, attacked the Legion for being "the self-appointed censor of a nation's progressive ideals," for bringing to the movies "the standard of narrow suppression, which from time immemorial has fought and blocked all forms of civilized progress."[2]

In Hollywood, Dudley Nichols, head of the Screen Writers' Guild, alleged that the Production Code Administration was making it impossible "to deal with the everyday scene of life around us."[3] Walter Wanger, producer, said the same thing: "Under this Code it was--and is--almost impossible to face and deal with the modern world."[4]

A negro daily has attributed to the Code the fact that films portray negroes in a disparaging light. "The Will Hays film code and that of the Catholics should now be gone over to remove barriers to fuller portrayal of American life."[5]

From the universities has come a charge that the Legion is obscurantist. Said one professor,

> There are two kinds of unsound ways of talking
> and writing about the movies. One of them is to
> ask only, "Is this movie entertaining?"...The other
> ... is the way of the Legion of Decency and similar
> organizations which ask only "Is there anything
> morally objectionable (according to our own standards
> of morality) in this picture?"[6]

----

1. Worth M. Tippy, New York Herald-tribune, March 5, 1937.
2. Film survey, August, 1938, quoted in "Report to the Episcopal Committee," 1938.
3. Box office, February 11, 1939.
4. Walter Wanger, New York Herald-tribune, February 26, 1939.
5. Pittsburgh Courier, May 30, 1942.
6. Professor Ernest Bernbaum, University of Illinois, Film daily, November 30, 1938.

Another has advocated the immediate abolition of the Hays office, the
Production Code, the Legion of Decency and all censorship organizations,
asserting that he "would rather take chance on sullying the great
American mind than stultifying it."[1]

In these and similar expressions of variance with the Legion,
there is evident a certain confusion between the Legion, the Code, the
Code Administration, and the policy of the industry leaders.

The policy of the industry has been to make pictures for
entertainment. "The special social function performed by the motion
picture industry is entertainment."[2] Slesinger properly observes
that Hays frequent references to the entertainment policy of the
industry "only means that in his judgment and in the judgment of his
colleagues entertainment pays. The sole function of the motion
picture is to make money."[3]

Since the film industry makes its pictures for sale to the widest
possible audiences, it would not be good business to risk the loss of
any substantial segment of the potential audience by challenging its
social convictions. Riegel notes that the movie industry and the radio
industry are alike in their insistence on producing entertainment
which will not alienate the loyalty of any part of their mass audiences.
"Both industries therefore show a desire to avoid controversial topics
and deny any obligation to change, criticize, or oppose the symbols
representing the least common denominator of popular acceptance."[4]

1. Professor Sawyer Falk, Syracuse University, The New York times,
   February 3, 1939.
2. Will H. Hays, "Films and society," The New York times, January 7,
   1945.
3. Donal Slesinger, "The film and public opinion," Print, radio and film
   in a democracy (ed. Douglas Waples), Chicago, The University of
   Chicago Press, 1942, p. 87.
4. O. W. Riegel, "Nationalism in press, radio and cinema," American
   sociological review, III (1938), 513.

The Production Code Administration seems to have gone further than the public pronouncements of industry leaders in the direction of restricting the critical functions of the movies. The facts are a matter of inter-industry debate. Walter Wanger said he had been restricted.[1] George J. Schaefer, president of R.K.O., challenged Wanger's statement.[2] Since the records of the Production Code Administration are not available as evidence, the dispute must be left unsettled.

The Production Code itself is another matter. There is no doubt that the Code says much about entertainment, little about social criticism. This in itself is not surprising, since the Code was drawn up on the basis of experience with the type of pictures which had been produced up to that time. In 1929 there was not much thought of making pictures with "social significance." On the other hand, there are no provisions in the Code which restrict the opportunity of making such pictures.

True, one of the "General Principles" of the Code states: "Law, natural or human, should not be ridiculed, nor shall sympathy be created for its violation." On the face of it, it might seem that this principle prohibits pictures which would aim at changing the law in the process of remedying social injustices.

The interpretation of this principle is found in the "Reasons Supporting" the provisions of the Code; the pertinent section reads as follows:

> By natural law is understood the law which is written in the hearts of all mankind, the great underlying principles

1. Wanger, loc. cit.
2. George J. Schaefer, Box office, March 4, 1939.

> of right and justice dictated by conscience.
> By human law is understood the law written by
> civilized nations.
> 1. The presentation of crimes against the law is
> often necessary for the carrying out of the plot.
> But the presentation must not throw sympathy for
> the crime against the law nor with the criminal
> as against those who punish him.
> 2. The courts of the land should not be presented
> as unjust. This does not mean that a single court
> may not be represented as unjust, much less that a
> single court official must not be presented this
> way. But the court system of the country must not
> suffer as a result of this presentation.

This section was undoubtedly conceived with reference to Westerns

and crime pictures which had shown a tendency to glorify outlaws and

criminals. It could scarcely have been in the minds of the framers

of the Code and of the industry heads who accepted it that these

provisions should prohibit films which would picture in an unfavorable

light such portions of the legal structure as might support social

inequities.

If there have been restrictions, then, they have not arisen from

the Code, but from within the industry or the Code Administration.

With these the Legion has no direct concern, except insofar as it, too,

does not exert pressure to change the status quo. Does the Legion,

therefore, put its stamp of approval on the existing social order?

Does it frown upon attempts to change it? The Legion's attitude in

this matter can be estimated from the record of its criticisms of the

films, from statements made by its leaders, and from the social

teachings of the Catholic Church.

The published lists of objections made by the Legion between

November 1939 and November 1943 show that the Legion objected twice

to films because of their attitude toward the Law. The first of these films was "The Letter," to which objection was made because of "disrespect for law;"[1] the second was "Roxy Hart," to which an objection was, "jibes at agencies of justice."[2] Neither of these films aimed at delivering a message of "social significance." On the other hand, during this same period, "Grapes of Wrath," a picture which packed a great deal of social criticism, was classified by the Legion "Unobjectionable for Adults."[3]

The record thus shows no reactionary evaluations from the Legion. Of course, this does not prove very much. Given the industry's policy, there were probably few, if any pictures made during this period which would give the Legion an opportunity to manifest a reactionary attitude, if it had one.

The statement made by Archbishop McNicholas in 1938 led some to believe that the Legion was being committed to social conservatism. The Archbishop announced that the Legion was opposed to the dissemination through the movies of "false, atheistic, and immoral doctrines repeatedly condemned by all accepted moral teachers."[4] His reference was obviously to Marxism, and to such other social theories as resemble Marxism in embodying an atheistic premise.

Those who identify social betterment with the acceptance of such theories are no doubt correct if they judge that the Legion of Decency stands ready to use its weight to reinforce the industry's policy of

1. Legion of Decency films reviewed, November 1940-November 1941, p. 26.
2. Legion of Decency films reviewed, November 1941-November 1942, p. 27.
3. Ibid., November 1939-November 1940, p. 20.
4. Press release, August 22, 1938.

not preaching these doctrines.

It would not, however, be a correct inference to conclude that the Legion is ready to threaten the production of all films which embody criticisms of the existing social order. The paramount norm of Legion policy in this matter is the social doctrine of the Catholic Church, which is authoritatively expressed in papal statements.

Pope Pius XI, in his encyclical letter On Motion Pictures, admitted the entertainment value of movies, but added,

> In addition to affording recreation, they are able...to communicate valuable conceptions,... to create at least the flavor of understanding among nations, social classes and races, to champion the cause of justice,...to contribute positively to the genesis of a just social order in the world.[1]

What the Pope meant by a "just social order" is well known to those who are familiar with the social encyclicals of the recent Popes. He who runs may read in them the sternest criticisms of the existing social orders.

Nor, it may be pointed out, does respect for legitimate authority preclude criticism of the political regime, Pius XII has made this clear:

> To express his own views of the duties and sacrifices that are imposed on him; not compelled to obey without being heard; these are two rights of the citizen which find in democracy, as its name implies, their expression.
> These multitudes,...are today firmly convinced ...that had there been the possibility of censuring and correcting the actions of public authority, the world would not have been dragged into the vortex of a disastrous war, and that to avoid for the future the repetition of such a catastrophe we must vest efficient guarantees in the people itself.[2]

[1] Pope Pius XI, On motion pictures, p. 9.
[2] Pope Pius XII, "Christmas message, 1944," The New York times, December 25, 1944.

"The Left," it may be concluded, has been misled as to the Legion's intentions and practice regarding pictures which deal with social criticism. Exception to this conclusion must be made in the case of those criticisms which have derived from sources hospitable to Marxism and similar social philosophies. In their case, the conflict seems to be irreconcilable.

Government Control?

The history of social control of the various forms of public entertainment has been such as to suggest the generalization, "the state has always been the agency through which reform groups have had to work for the regulation of amusements."[1] In the United States, the Watch and Ward Society of New England, the New York Society for the Suppression of Vice, the Anti-Saloon League, and other groups pressuring for "reform" have almost invariably directed their pressure toward the imposition of their ideal patterns through the police power of the state.

The Legion, as has been seen, broke with this tradition. It eschewed federal censorship and maintained a hands-off policy regarding the enactment of federal legislation to improve movie morals through the elimination of block-booking and other trade practices. The Legion has directed its pressure immediately to the motion picture industry, which exercises authoritative control over its own product. Thus, in the total control system, the state is completely by-passed.

There are many divergent proposals regarding the most suitable position of the government in the control process. We shall consider

1. Ida Craven, "Public amusements," Encyclopedia of the social sciences, II, p. 45.

the most important of them, and their implications for the future of
the Legion of Decency.

Proponents of Government Control

The extreme form of state control of motion pictures is found in
the totalitarian states, especially Germany and the Soviet Union. In
these two countries all cultural activities are managed by the state in
such a way that not only is there the negative process of eliminating
unacceptable cultural products, but there is also positive interference
by which the state imposes definite trends on cultural activity and
tries to shape the mentality of its subjects.[1]

In the United States there has been little advocacy of the totalitarian brand of governmental control of the movies. Mrs. Robbins
Gilman's tour of the country in 1934 proposing such control did not
enlist a perceptible following.[2]

There have been, however, and there still are, those who favor a
less drastic form of state control. The professional reformers of pre-
Legion days wanted federal censorship. Their activities have terminated.
A different sort of group, the Motion Picture Research Council, which
sponsored the Payne Fund Studies in 1932 and 1933, still favors federal
regulation. In substance, such proposals would replace the Production
Code Administration with a federal agency doing the same work.

----

1. Timasheff, "The legal regimentation of culture in National Socialist
Germany," Fordham law review, XI (1942), 1 f; Derrick Sington and
Arthur Weidenfelc, The Goebbels experiment, New Haven, Yale University Press, 1942, chap. ix, "The cinema in the Third Reich." On the
cinema in Soviet Russia, vide Philip E. Mosely, "Freedom of artistic
expression and scientific enquiry in Russia," The annals, CC (1938),
254-274; Samuel N. Harper, Making Bolsheviks, Chicago, The University
of Chicago Press, 1931, pp. 109, 139; Roger N. Baldwin, Liberty under
the Soviets, New York, The Vanguard Press, 1929, pp. 154 ff; cf. Max
Eastman, Artists in uniform, New York, Alfred A. Knopf, 1934.
2. Supra, p. 137.

How would the change from self-regulation to governmental regulation affect the Legion of Decency?

A federal commission, not in the pay of the film industry, would not be influenced by the box-office pressure of the Legion. Should the federal agency prove to be more lenient than the Production Code Administration with regard to those values which are the special concern of the Legion, producers would probably be tempted to "get away with" pictures which would violate the Legion's standards. The Legion's non-Catholic support might conceivably be weakened if there were a conflict for recognition between the values of the government's agency and those of the Legion. Catholics would presumably be more constant in their adherence to the values which are sanctioned for them by their consciences formed by the Church's religious teaching. After an initial period of confusion, should the Legion maintain its following, the producers would likely be forced to reintroduce some form of self-control to protect themselves from further financial loss. In such an event, the situation of the Legion would not be unlike that of the present.

Likewise, should the values of the federal agency prove to be in substantial agreement with the Legion's value system, the present status of the Legion would be maintained. In neither case would it be likely that the Legion would abandon its activites.

Opponents of Government Control

The extreme position in this camp is that of those who would abolish all formal social constraints upon the movies, of whatever

nature.[1] They would eliminate not only censorship and self-regulation
and Legion of Decency pressure, but also the existing legal provisions
for punishing the sponsors of indecent and improper entertainment.
Their argument is that since there is lack of agreement concerning the
definition of obscenity and similar expressions, there is, therefore,
no reality in the existential order to which the terms refer. There
are few who express themselves in agreement with this position.

More common is the expression of a desire to see all formal
controls abolished except that of the state's police power which is
to be invoked only in particular cases of emergency, after the offense.[2]
The pet hate of this group is censorship by previous restraint, no
matter by whom it is exercised. Chaffee, best known for his advocacy
of free speech, has applied his principle to the films:

> It would seem that the informal control by
> audiences would be sufficient, in view of their
> power by voluntary boycotts to ruin both the
> producer and the theater if really objectionable
> pictures are forced on them. Furthermore, if the
> films are clearly filthy, both these responsible
> persons can readily be punished by state and
> federal prosecutions.[3]

Fraenkel concurs in this opinion,[4] as do many who conceive the cases
of the motion picture and the press to be parallel, the alternatives
being censorship or relatively complete freedom of expression.

1. Morris L. Ernst and William Seagle, To the pure, New York, The
   Viking Press, 1928; Morris L. Ernst, Censored: the private life of
   the movies, New York, J. Capehart and H. Smith, 1930; Morris L.
   Ernst and Alexander Lindey, The censor marches on, New York,
   Doubleday, Doran and Company, 1940. Cf. Horace M. Kallen, Indecency
   and the seven arts, New York, Horace Liveright, 1930, pp. 31 f.
2. Such a policy would be characteristic of the ideal type of liberal
   society constructed by Timasheff, Fordham law review, loc. cit.
3. Zechariah Chaffee, Jr., Free speech in the United States, Cambridge,
   Harvard University Press, 1941, p. 542.
4. Osmond K. Fraenkel, Our civil liberties, New York, The Viking Press
   1944, pp. 104 f.

This group, unlike the next to be considered, does not propose to modify the structure of the film industry. To all intents and purposes, they propose a return to the situation which existed before the Legion of Decency without the state and municipal censorship which was then in use. Without entering into detailed discussion of the dubious effectiveness of legal prosecution as the sole instrument of control of the films: the vagueness of the legal tests of obscenity,[1] and the fact that statutes can hardly lay down more than the most general standards,[2] it may be pointed out that there was dissatisfaction with the proposed system in the past; it is doubtful that society would permit the return of that situation.

Another group pins most of its faith upon loosening the grasp upon production control which is at present in the hands of a few major producers. In this connection, Walter Lippmann has written:

> Until recently the method of reform has been to impose certain moral standards on the producers by a combination of legal censorship and organized boycotts. It is evident, I think, that this method has not been successful....Within the obvious limits of the ordinary law about obscenity and provocation to crime, the best regulation would be that exercised by the customers at the box office of a theater.
> ...The remedy...is not to impose standards on the existing monopolistic corporations, but by invoking the anti-trust laws and perhaps new legislation to break their power.[3]

With the monopoly broken, the argument runs, independent producers will be able to produce pictures on moderate budgets. The need for mass audiences will be eliminated. Pictures will be made for differentiated audiences. There will then be no need for regulating the content, by

1. Chaffee, op. cit., pp. 150 f.
2. Ibid., p. 531.
3. Walter Lippmann, "The morals of the movies," New York Herald-tribune, November 12, 1935.

the government or by the industry. The only control will be informal audience control and the post-factum restraints contained in the existing legal code.

The Department of Justice has tried to break up the monopoly of the film industry. Should it carry its attack to the point where it would force the dissolution of the Hays office, the Legion of Decency would face a situation frought with real problems. Instead of a single focus for its pressure, the Hays office, it would have as many as there are producers. There is no way of knowing what structural changes the Legion would introduce to accomodate itself to this new situation.

It should be noted, however, that the Department of Justice did not include the Production Code Administration within the scope of its charges, and that few complaints have been made by independent producers regarding the activities of that agency.[1] Pressure for the proposed change, then, does not seem likely to come from within the industry; nor, in the relatively quiet state of public opinion on the movies, is it likely to come from popular demand. Pressure against industry self-control is more likely to be accompanied by pressure for governmental control, under the inspiration of that political philosophy which leads the authors of the TNEC monograph to ask what assurance there can be that control over the moral standards of the films "will always be wisely exercised by a nongovernmental group?"[2]

---

1. The motion picture industry--a pattern of control, p. 66.
2. Ibid.

The Autonomy of the Control System

The existing system of social control of movie morals, with authoritative control vested in the Hays office supported by social pressure coming from the Legion of Decency, is an autonomous exercise of power. The entire process is carried on outside the sphere of the police power of the state. This situation raises certain questions. From the viewpoint of the state, is this an encroachment upon the state's power system? From the viewpoint of the Church, is industrial self-regulation a policy consonant with her social philosophy? From the viewpoint of Church-State relations, does the adoption of this autonomous system of control possess any significance?

The State Power System

The first of these questions may be answered with despatch. First, it may be pointed out that the state has no monopoly on the use of power.[1] Merriam has shown the extent to which the family, the church, economic groups, ethnic groups and many others exercise power.[2]

Second, as has been noted previously, it is impossible to mark out with exactness the respective boundaries of the state and other associations merely on the basis of function.[3] The state's functions overlap those of the other associations at one or other point of contact.

Groups which exercise power and are not immediately under the management of the state while they do so, are not automatically

1. The use of power should not be confused with the use of physical force. The latter "is compulsion in its purest unconditional form, and in civilized communities it is vested as a right in the state." R. M. MacIver, Society: a textbook of sociology, New York, Farrar and Rinehart, 1937, p. 342. Emphasis in original.
2. Merriam, Political power, pp. 47-85.
3. Supra, p. 118.

considered to be encroaching upon the preserves of the state, nor are they considered to be usurping the functions of the state, except by the proponents of totalitarian ideologies.

The state's position with regard to these other associations, as far as power and function are concerned, is well summarized in Timasheff's description of the political power structure as "a generalized (not specialized) system with an independent 'supreme' active center."[1] Such a system does not exclude the autonomous use of power by specialized groups such as those considered here. The Hays office control and the Legion of Decency pressure are not usurpers of state prerogatives.

Industry Self-control and Catholic Social Theory

Contemporary Catholic social theory is opposed to the totalitarian system of direct state control over all phases of human life. To the totalitarian system it opposes the "principle of subsidiarity."[2] This principle maintains that the State should devote itself to those tasks only which individuals or subordinate groups cannot fulfill by their own power. Writing in a context which had particular reference to economic associations, Pius XI explained the principle in the following words:

> Just as it is wrong to withdraw from the individual
> and commit to the community at large what private enter-
> prise and industry can accomplish, so too it is an

---

1. Timasheff, Sociology of law, p. 218.
2. Harold F. Trehey, Foundations of a modern guild system, Washington, D.C., The Catholic University of America Press, 1940, pp. 47-52.

> injustice, a grave evil and a disturbance of right
> order for a larger and higher organization to
> arrogate to itself functions which can be performed
> efficiently by smaller and lower bodies.[1]

It was partly on this ground that the same Pope condemned the excessively

bureaucratic and political character of the Fascist "corporations" as

being apt to serve "particular political aims rather than contributing

to the initiation of a better social order."[2]

It cannot be maintained that the decision of the Legion of Decency

to go along with the Hays office self-regulation was a conscious appli-

cation of the theoretical principle of subsidiarity. The anti-

stateism implied in this principle stems ultimately from the recog-

nition of the family and other groups as prior to the state; but its

modern application has been principally to the economic sphere. It is

doubtful that the Bishops were thinking of it when they preferred

industry self-control to state control. But it was certainly the

persuasion of the Episcopal Committee that by avoiding federal

censorship they were making it less likely that control of movie

morals would be serving "particular political aims rather than contri-

buting to the initiation of a better social order."

Industrial self-regulation is consonant with Catholic social

theory. Were the motion picture industry organized in such wise that

employee as well as employer were represented in its highest council,

and were the organization broadened to include all rather than merely

---

1. Pope Pius XI, Forty years after, reconstructing the social order,
   Washington, D.C., National Catholic Welfare Conference, 1936, p. 26.
2. Ibid., p. 30.

the most powerful members of the industry, its self-regulatory system would be more completely in accord with the goals of Catholic social philosophy.

Church and State

From the viewpoint of Church-State relations, the activities of the Legion of Decency exemplify a possibly significant phase of development.

Both Church and State exercise power. Sturzo calls this duality of power a "diarchy."[1] The structure of this diarchy has changed in the course of historical development. The prevailing mode today is the "individualistic" diarchy, wherein the power of the Church, which is separated from the secular or laic state, is "mainly expressed as a spiritual power over the faithful as individuals, and no longer in an authoritative and juridical form over States."[2]

Although the Church is legally heteronomous to the State, She exercises "directive power"[3] over the State insofar as she appeals to the consciences of the faithful, who as citizens influence the direction of the state's exercise of power, or even oppose it in the name of Christian morality. Such directive power is exercised when churchmen urge support for plans to organize international society.

1. Luigi Sturzo, Essai de sociologie, Paris, 1937, p. 203, quoted in Luigi Sturzo, Church and state, New York, Longsmans, Green and Company, 1939, p. 46, n. 1, "By diarchy we mean the formation of two powers, either within each group or in the social complexus as as a whole. The diarchy of which we are speaking is of a sociological character, whether it comes about on the political plane or on other planes of society."
2. Sturzo, Church and state, p. 547.
3. Ibic., p. 551.

It is exercised when churchmen tell the faithful not to obey anti-
semitic laws. It is a power making itself felt through pressure,
rather than through direct, authoritarian control over the state.

Similar power, however, may be exercised within the community,
without any reference to the state. In an unorganized way this power
has been exercised continuously through the history of the Church
inasmuch as the Church has always urged personal conformity to its
moral code. The organization of this power, without reference to the
state, is a modern phenomenon. In Europe such groups organized for
the attainment of spiritual and moral objectives by non-political
means are known as "Catholic Action" groups. In the United States
the organization of such groups has not made much progress. But the
Legion of Decency is a specialized example of the generic type.

The technique of the Legion of Decency has been imitated in
Europe and in Latin America.[1] Usually, in these countries, it has been
incorporated into the existing Catholic Action groups. The state, in
most of these countries, censored motion pictures, but chiefly for the
elimination of politically objectionable content. The Church has
organized pressure groups, similar to the Legion, to eliminate morally
objectionable content, without reference to the political censorship.

In the medieval community, had the motion picture problem arisen,
the morals of the movies would have been immediately subject to
ecclesiastical supervision, whose enforcement would have been in the
hands of the state. In the community of today, the morals of the

---

1. Felix A. Morlion, O.P., The apostolate of public opinion, Montreal,
   Fides, 1944, p. 62.

movies are directly subject to the industry's own supervision, while
the Church appeals to the conscience of the faithful to refuse
patronage to objectionable films, offering a prudential guide for
their discrimination. The result, as long as the consciences of
the Church members recognize the Church code of morals, is that the
production of objectionable pictures is made unprofitable.

In both systems, the medieval and the modern, the objective of
morally unobjectionable films is obtained. In the modern system the
hazards of confusion between moral and political values are minimized.
If the author may be permitted the luxury of bringing this study to
an end with the expression of a value judgment, he would use the
privilege to say that the system of directive control through the
community seems a distinct improvement over direct control through
the state.

BIBLIOGRAPHY

Books

Allport, Gordon W.: Personality, New York, Henry Holt and Company, 1937.

Aquinas, St. Thomas: De regimine principum ad regem Cypri et de regimine Judaeorum ad ducissam Brabantiae, Taurini, Marietti, Joseph Mathis Curante, 1924.

--- : Summa theologica (ed. altera Romana), 3 vols., Romae, n.d.

Baldwin, Roger N.: Liberty under the Soviets, New York, The Vanguard Press, 1929.

Bernard, L. L.: Social control, New York, The Macmillan Company, 1939.

Bonney, Merle E.: Techniques of appeal and of social control, Ph.D. dissertation, Columbia University, 1934.

Brown, B. Warren: Social groups, Chicago, The Fairthorn Company, 1926.

Cantril, Hadley: The psychology of social movements, New York, John Wiley and Sons, 1941.

Chaffee, Zechariah, Jr.: Free speech in the United States, Cambridge, Harvard University Press, 1941.

Chase, Stuart: Democracy under pressure, New York, The Twentieth Century Fund, 1945.

Cicognani, Amleto Giovanni: Canon law. Translated by Joseph M. O'Hara and Francis Brennan. Philadelphia, The Dolphin Press, 1934.

Coyle, Grace L.: Social process in organized groups, New York, John Wiley and Sons, 1932.

Dowd, Jerome: Control in human societies, New York, D. Appleton-Century Company, Inc., 1936.

Eastman, Max: Artists in uniform, New York, Alfred A. Knopf, 1934.

Ernst, Morris L.: Censored: the private life of the movies, New York, J. Capehart and H. Smith, 1930.

--- , and Lindey, Alexander: The censor marches on, New York, Doubleday, Doran and Company, 1940.

--- , and Seagle, William: To the pure, New York, The Viking Press, 1928.

Eubank, Earle E.: The concepts of sociology, New York, D. C. Heath and Company, 1932.

Film facts 1942, New York, Motion Picture Producers and Distributors of America, Inc., 1942.

Fraenkel, Osmond K.: Our civil liberties, New York, The Viking Press, 1944.

Gillin, John L., and Gillin, John P.: An introduction to sociology, New York, The Macmillan Company, 1942.

Hankins, Frank H.: An introduction to the study of society, (rev. ed.), New York, The Macmillan Company, 1935.

Harper, Samuel N.: Making Bolsheviks, Chicago, The University of Chicago Press, 1931.

Hays, Will H.: See and hear, Motion Picture Producers and Distributors of America, Inc., 1929.

International motion picture almanac, 1944-45, New York, Quigley Publishing Company, Inc., 1945.

Kallen, Horace: Indecency and the seven arts, New York, Horace Liveright, 1930.

Landis, Paul H.: Social control, Philadelphia, J. B. Lippincott Company, 1939.

Linton, Ralph: The study of man, New York, D. Appleton-Century Company, 1936.

Lumley, Frederick E.: Means of social control, New York, The Century Company, 1925.

Lyons, Eugene: The Red decade, Indianapolis, The Bobbs-Merrill Company, 1941.

MacIver, R. M.: Social causation, Boston, Ginn and Company, 1942.

--- : Society: a textbook of sociology, New York, Farrar and Rinehart, 1937.

Martin, Olga, J.: Hollywood's movie commandments, New York, The H. W. Wilson Company, 1937.

Merriam, Charles E.: Political power, New York, Whittlesey House, McGraw-Hill Book Company, 1934.

--- : Public and private government, New Haven, Yale University Press, 1944.

Morlion, Felix A.: The apostolate of public opinion, Montreal, Fides, 1944.

The motion picture industry--a pattern of control, U.S. Congress, Temporary National Economic Committee, Monograph No. 43, Washington, D.C., Government Printing Office, 1941.

Murchison, Carl (ed.): A handbook of social psychology, Worcester, Clark University Press, 1935.

Ogburn, William F., and Nimkoff, Meyer F.: Sociology, Boston, Houghton and Mifflin Company, 1940.

Park, Robert E., and Burgess, Ernest W.: Introduction to the science of sociology, Chicago, The University of Chicago Press, 1921.

Parsons, Talcott: The structure of social action, New York, McGraw-Hill Book Company, 1937.

Perlman, William J. (ed.): The movies on trial, New York, The Macmillan Company, 1936.

Pernicone, Joseph M.: The ecclesiastical prohibition of books, Washington, D.C., Catholic University of America, 1932.

Perry, Ralph Barton: General theory of value, New York, Longmans, Green and Company, 1926.

Pius XI, Pope: Encyclical letter on motion pictures, translated, Washington, D.C., National Catholic Welfare Conference, 1936.

--- : Forty years after, reconstructing the social order, translated, Washington, D.C., National Catholic Welfare Conference, 1936.

Pound, Roscoe: Social control through law, New Haven, Yale University Press, 1942.

Putnam, George Haven: The censorship of the Roman Catholic Church, 2 vols., New York, G. P. Putnam's Sons, 1906-1907.

Quigley, Martin: Decency in motion pictures, New York, The Macmillan Company, 1937.

Ramsaye, Terry: A million and one nights, 2 vols, New York, Simon and Schuster, 1926.

Reuter, Edward B.: Handbook of sociology, New York, The Dryden Press, 1941.

Ross, Edward A.: Social control, New York, The Macmillan Company, 1901.

Seldes, Gilbert: The movies come from America, New York, Charles Scribner's Sons, 1937.

Sherif, M.: The psychology of social norms, New York, Harper and Brothers, 1936.

Sington, Derrick, and Weidenfeld, Arthur: The Goebbels experiment, New Haven, Yale University Press, 1943.

Sturzo, Luigi: Church and state, New York, Longmans, Green and Company, 1939.

Sutherland, Robert L., and Woodward, Julian L.: Introductory sociology (2d ed.), Philadelphia, J. B. Lippincott Company, 1940.

Thorp, Margaret F.: America at the movies, New Haven, Yale University Press, 1939.

Timasheff, N. S.: An introduction to the sociology of law, Cambridge, Harvard University Committee on Research in the Social Sciences, 1939.

Trehey, Harold F.: Foundations of a modern guild system, Washington, D.C., The Catholic University of America Press, 1940.

Tufts, James H.: America's social morality, New York, Henry Holt and Company, 1933.

Waller, Willard: The family: a dynamic interpretation, New York, The Dryden Press, 1939.

Waples, Douglas (ed.): Print, radio and film in a democracy, Chicago, The University of Chicago Press, 1942.

Williams, Michael: The Catholic Church in action, New York, The Macmillan Company, 1934.

Young, Donald R.: Motion pictures, a study in social legislation, Ph.D. dissertation, University of Pennsylvania, 1922.

Young, Kimball: Sociology, a study of society and culture, New York, American Book Company, 1942.

Documents and Reports

Federal Council of the Churches of Christ in America, The public relations of the motion picture industry, a report by the Department of Research and Education, New York, 1931.

Legion of Decency films reviewed, feature motion pictures reviewed by the New York office of the National Legion of Decency. Annual list of ratings. New York, National Legion of Decency, since 1937.

Motion Picture Producers and Distributors of America, Inc., "A code to govern the making of talking, synchronized and silent motion pictures," (mimeographed), n.d.

Motion Picture Producers and Distributors of America, Inc.: "A code to maintain social and community values in the production of silent, synchronized and talking motion pictures," n.d.

--- : "Production code and uniform interpretation," n.d.

--- : Rule 21 of the code of the motion picture industry, New York, n.d.

National Board of Censorship of Motion Pictures: Report of the National Board of Censorship of Motion Pictures, New York, 1911 and annually through 1916.

U. S. Congress, House: "The Patman Bill," H. 6097. 73d Congress.

U. S. Congress, Senate: "The Neely-Pettingill Bill," S. 3012. 74th Congress.

Articles

Bain, Read: Review of Landis, Social control, American sociological review, IV (1939), 732-734.

Barnes, Howard: New York Herald-tribune, April 26, 1940.

Bierstedt, Robert: "The means-end schema in sociological theory," American sociological review, III (1938), 665-671.

Boyle, Hugh C.: "The Legion of Decency a permanent campaign," Ecclesiastical review, XCI (1934), 367-370.

Burgess, J. Stewart: "The study of modern social movements as a means for clarifying the process of social action," Social forces, XXII (1944), 269-275.

Childs, Harwood L.: The annals, CLXXIX (May, 1935), xi-xii.

Chotzinoff, Samuel: "Words without music," New York post, July 9, 1934.

Churchill, Douglas W.: "Hollywood discovers that virtue pays," The New York times magazine, January 20, 1935.

Coyle, Matthew A.: "The Church and the theatre," Ecclesiastical review, XCII (1935),561-577, XCIII (1935), 12-28, 133-142.

Craven, Ida: "Public amusements," Encyclopedia of the social sciences, II, pp. 39-46.

Crisler, R.: The New York times, April 26, 1940.

Crowther, Bosley: The New York times, November 16, 1941.

Dictionary of sociology: articles, "Pressure groups," "Social control."

Dinkel, Robert M.: "Attitudes of children toward supporting aged parents," American sociological review, IX (1944), 370-379.

Fidler, Jimmie: Worcester evening gazette, December 2, 1944.

Folsom, J. K.: "Changing values in sex and family relations," American sociological review, II (1937), 717-726.

Folsom, Joseph K., and Strelsky, Nikander: "Russian values and character--a preliminary exploration," American sociological review, IX (1944), 296-307.

Gillet, M. S.: "Theatre," Dictionnaire apologetique de la foi catholique, Paris, Gabriel Beauchesne, 1928, t. iv, cols. 617-619.

Girerd, Francois: "Theatre et cinema--I. Morale," Dictionnaire pratique des connaissances religieuses, Paris, Libraire Letouzey et Ane, 1928, t. xvi, cols. 1633-1635.

Harding, Francis A.: "More blessed to get!" The American scholar, VIII (1938-1939), 35-44.

Hart, Hornell: "Function," Dictionary of sociology, p. 125.

--- : "Structure," Dictionary of sociology, p. 310.

Hays, Will H.: "Films and society," The New York times, January 7, 1945.

Hopper, Hedda: Worcester daily telegram, December 2, 1944.

Kadin, Theodore: "Administrative censorship: a study of the mails, motion pictures and radio broadcasting," Boston University law review, XIX (1939), 533-585.

Kluckhohn, Clyde: "The place of theory in anthropological studies," Philosophy of science, VI (1939), 328-344.

Knight, Eric: "The movie 'czar'," Philadelphia evening public ledger, August 25, 1934.

Laidler, Harry W.: "Boycott," Encyclopedia of the social sciences, II, pp. 662-666.

Lasswell, Harold D.: "Censorship," Encyclopedia of the social sciences, III, pp. 290-294.

Lemert, Edwin M.: "The folkways and social control," American sociological review, VII (1942), 394-399.

Lippmann, Walter: "The morals of the movies," New York Herald tribune, November 12, 1935.

MacGregor, Ford H.: "Official censorship legislation," The annals, CXXVIII (November, 1926), 163-174.

MacIver, R. M.: "Social pressures," Encyclopedia of the social sciences, XII, pp. 344-348.

McNicholas, John T.: "The Episcopal Committee and the problem of evil motion pictures," Ecclesiastical review, XCI (1934), 113-119.

Mosely, Philip E.: "Freedom of artistic expression and scientific enquiry in Russia," The annals, CC (1938), 254-274.

Mowrer, Ernest R.: "Methodological problems in social disorganization," American sociological review, VI (1941), 829-849.

Parsons, Wilfrid: "A code for motion pictures," America, XLIII (April 19, 1930), 32-33.

--- : "Motion picture morality," America, XLIV (November 15, 1930), 131-133.

Pius XII, Pope: "Christmas message," The New York times, December 25, 1944.

Riegel, O. W.: "Nationalism in press. radio and cinema," American sociological review, III (1938), 510-515.

Stanley, Fred: The New York times, November 19, 1944.

Timasheff, N. S.: "Cultural order in liberal, fascist and communist society," The American Catholic sociological review, III (1942), 63-71.

--- : "The legal regimentation of culture in National Socialist Germany," Fordham law review, XI (1942), 1-29.

Turnell, Martin: "Cinema in society," Blackfriars, XIX (1938), 571-588.

Wilkinson, Lupton A.: Photoplay, September, 1937.

Willey, Malcolm: "Communication agencies and the volume of propaganda," The annals, CLXXIX (May, 1935), 194-200.

The Yale law journal, "Censorship of motion pictures," XLIX (1939), 87-113.

Pamphlets

Exhibitors of motion pictures and the National Board of Censorship, New York, n.d.
Handbook of the National Catholic War Council, Washington, D.C., 1918.

How to judge the morality of motion pictures. "A popular guide to
    right standards in motion picture entertainment, authorized by the
    Episcopal Committee on motion pictures for the Legion of Decency,"
    Washington, D.C., National Catholic Welfare Conference, n.d.

Lord, Daniel A., S.J.: The motion pictures betray America, St. Louis,
    The Queen's Work, Inc., 1934.

The National Board of Review of Motion Pictures--how it works, New York,
    n.d.

The National Catholic Welfare Conference, Washington, D.C., n.d.

Skinner, Richard Dana: "The morals of the screen," Washington, D.C.,
    National Catholic Welfare Conference, reprinted from The Catholic
    educational review, October, 1935.

                              Newspapers

Boston evening American

Los Angeles Times

New York Herald tribune

New York Post

The New York times

New York World-telegram

L'Osservatore Romano

Philadelphia inquirer-public ledger

Philadelphia evening public ledger

Pittsburgh Courier

Washington Star

Worcester daily telegram

Worcester evening gazette

                              Periodicals

America

The Catholic news, New York

Christian century

Fortune

Literary digest

The nation

The new republic

Saturday review of literature

Trade Journals

Box office

Cue

Exhibitors' film exchange

Exhibitors' herald

Motion picture daily

Motion picture herald

Variety

Unpublished Material

"Confidential memorandum to dioceses and diocesan organizations of
     the Legion of Decency." From the New York office of the Legion
     of Decency, September 21, 1944.

Inglis, Ruth A.: "The Hays office control of motion picture content,"
     Ph.D. dissertation, Bryn Mawr, 1945.

Janes, Robert W.: "The Legion of Decency and the motion picture
     industry," M.A. dissertation, University of Chicago, 1939.

Letter: Breen, Joseph I., to Parsons, Wilfrid, August 11, 1933.

Letter: Chase, Wm. Sheafe, to McNicholas, John T., April 2, 1934.

Letter: Dinneen, F. G., to Parsons, Wilfrid, July 12, 1933.

Letter: Irwin, Theodore, to McClafferty, John J., June 2, 1938.

Letter: Looram, Mrs. James F., to (confidential), February 14, 1935.

Letter: Looram, Mrs. James F., to (confidential), March 2, 1938.

Letter: McClafferty, John J., to (confidential), February 17, 1938.

Letter: McClafferty, John J., to (confidential), April 13, 1938.

Letter, McNicholas, John T., to Moore, Edward R., November 11, 1936.

Letter: Parsons, Wilfrid, to Hayes, Patrick Cardinal, July 17, 1930.

Letter: Parsons, Wilfrid, to Lord, Daniel A., March 15, 1930.

Letter: Parsons, Wilfrid, to Quigley, Martin, March 7, 1932.

Letter: Quigley, Martin, to Breen, Joseph I., February 21, 1938.

Letter: Quigley, Martin, to Hays, Will H., August 14, 1931.

"Notes," sent to Bishops by the Episcopal Committee on Motion Pictures, May 16, 1934.

"Report of the Episcopal Committee on Motion Pictures," 1935.

"Report to the Episcopal Committee on Motion Pictures," made annually by the Executive Secretary of the National Legion of Decency.

The Arno Press Cinema Program

THE LITERATURE OF CINEMA

Series I & II

Agate, James. **Around Cinemas.** 1946.

Agate, James. **Around Cinemas.** (Second Series). 1948.

American Academy of Political and Social Science. **The Motion Picture in Its Economic and Social Aspects,** edited by Clyde L. King. **The Motion Picture Industry,** edited by Gordon S. Watkins. *The Annals,* November, 1926/1927.

L'Art Cinematographique, Nos. 1-8. 1926-1931.

Balcon, Michael, Ernest Lindgren, Forsyth Hardy and Roger Manvell. **Twenty Years of British Film, 1925-1945.** 1947.

Bardèche, Maurice and Robert Brasillach. **The History of Motion Pictures,** edited by Iris Barry. 1938.

Benoit-Levy, Jean. **The Art of the Motion Picture.** 1946.

Blumer, Herbert. **Movies and Conduct.** 1933.

Blumer, Herbert and Philip M. Hauser. **Movies, Delinquency, and Crime.** 1933.

Buckle, Gerard Fort. **The Mind and the Film.** 1926.

Carter, Huntly. **The New Spirit in the Cinema.** 1930.

Carter, Huntly. **The New Spirit in the Russian Theatre, 1917-1928.** 1929.

Carter, Huntly. **The New Theatre and Cinema of Soviet Russia.** 1924.

Charters, W. W. **Motion Pictures and Youth.** 1933.

Cinema Commission of Inquiry. **The Cinema: Its Present Position and Future Possibilities.** 1917.

Dale, Edgar. **Children's Attendance at Motion Pictures.** Dysinger, Wendell S. and Christian A. Ruckmick. **The Emotional Responses of Children to the Motion Picture Situation.** 1935.

Dale, Edgar. **The Content of Motion Pictures.** 1935.

Dale, Edgar. **How to Appreciate Motion Pictures.** 1937.

Dale, Edgar, Fannie W. Dunn, Charles F. Hoban, Jr., and Etta Schneider. **Motion Pictures in Education: A Summary of the Literature.** 1938.

Davy, Charles. **Footnotes to the Film.** 1938.

Dickinson, Thorold and Catherine De la Roche. **Soviet Cinema.** 1948.

Dickson, W. K. L., and Antonia Dickson. **History of the Kinetograph, Kinetoscope and Kinetophonograph.** 1895.

Forman, Henry James. **Our Movie Made Children.** 1935.

Freeburg, Victor Oscar. **The Art of Photoplay Making.** 1918.

Freeburg, Victor Oscar. **Pictorial Beauty on the Screen.** 1923.

Hall, Hal, editor. **Cinematographic Annual,** 2 vols. 1930/1931.

Hampton, Benjamin B. **A History of the Movies.** 1931.

Hardy, Forsyth. **Scandinavian Film.** 1952.

Hepworth, Cecil M. **Animated Photography: The A B C of the Cinematograph.** 1900.

Hoban, Charles F., Jr., and Edward B. Van Ormer. **Instructional Film Research 1918-1950.** 1950.

Holaday, Perry W. and George D. Stoddard. **Getting Ideas from the Movies.** 1933.

Hopwood, Henry V. **Living Pictures.** 1899.

Hulfish, David S. **Motion-Picture Work.** 1915.

Hunter, William. **Scrutiny of Cinema.** 1932.

Huntley, John. **British Film Music.** 1948.

Irwin, Will. **The House That Shadows Built.** 1928.

Jarratt, Vernon. **The Italian Cinema.** 1951.

Jenkins, C. Francis. **Animated Pictures.** 1898.

Lang, Edith and George West. **Musical Accompaniment of Moving Pictures.** 1920.

London, Kurt. **Film Music.** 1936.

Lutz, E [dwin] G [eorge]. **The Motion-Picture Cameraman.** 1927.

Manvell, Roger. **Experiment in the Film.** 1949.

Marey, Etienne Jules. **Movement.** 1895.

Martin, Olga J. **Hollywood's Movie Commandments.** 1937.

Mayer, J. P. **Sociology of Film: Studies and Documents.** 1946. New Introduction by J. P. Mayer.

Münsterberg, Hugo. **The Photoplay: A Psychological Study.** 1916.
Nicoll, Allardyce. **Film and Theatre.** 1936.

Noble, Peter. **The Negro in Films.** 1949.

Peters, Charles C. **Motion Pictures and Standards of Morality.** 1933.

Peterson, Ruth C. and L. L. Thurstone. **Motion Pictures and the Social Attitudes of Children.** Shuttleworth, Frank K. and Mark A. May. **The Social Conduct and Attitudes of Movie Fans.** 1933.

Phillips, Henry Albert. **The Photodrama.** 1914.

Photoplay Research Society. **Opportunities in the Motion Picture Industry.** 1922.

Rapée, Erno. **Encyclopaedia of Music for Pictures.** 1925.

Rapée, Erno. **Motion Picture Moods for Pianists and Organists.** 1924.

Renshaw, Samuel, Vernon L. Miller and Dorothy P. Marquis. **Children's Sleep.** 1933.

Rosten, Leo C. **Hollywood: The Movie Colony, The Movie Makers.** 1941.

Sadoul, Georges. **French Film.** 1953.

Screen Monographs I, 1923-1937. 1970.

Screen Monographs II, 1915-1930. 1970.

Sinclair, Upton. **Upton Sinclair Presents William Fox.** 1933.

Talbot, Frederick A. **Moving Pictures.** 1912.

Thorp, Margaret Farrand. **America at the Movies.** 1939.

Wollenberg, H. H. **Fifty Years of German Film.** 1948.

RELATED BOOKS AND PERIODICALS

Allister, Ray. **Friese-Greene: Close-Up of an Inventor.** 1948.

Art in Cinema: A Symposium of the Avant-Garde Film, edited by Frank Stauffacher. 1947.

The Art of Cinema: Selected Essays. New Foreword by George Amberg. 1971.

Balázs, Béla. **Theory of the Film.** 1952.

Barry, Iris. **Let's Go to the Movies.** 1926.

de Beauvoir, Simone. **Brigitte Bardot and the Lolita Syndrome.** 1960.

Carrick, Edward. **Art and Design in the British Film.** 1948.

Close Up. Vols. 1-10, 1927-1933 (all published).

Cogley, John. **Report on Blacklisting. Part I: The Movies.** 1956.

Eisenstein, S. M. **Que Viva Mexico!** 1951.

Experimental Cinema. 1930-1934 (all published).

Feldman, Joseph and Harry. **Dynamics of the Film.** 1952.

Film Daily Yearbook of Motion Pictures. Microfilm, 18 reels, 35 mm. 1918-1969.

Film Daily Yearbook of Motion Pictures. 1970.

Film Daily Yearbook of Motion Pictures. (Wid's Year Book). 3 vols., 1918-1922.

The Film Index: A Bibliography. Vol. I: The Film as Art. 1941.

Film Society Programmes. 1925-1939 (all published).

Films: A Quarterly of Discussion and Analysis. Nos. 1-4, 1939-1940 (all published).

Flaherty, Frances Hubbard. **The Odyssey of a Film-Maker: Robert Flaherty's Story.** 1960.

General Bibliography of Motion Pictures, edited by Carl Vincent, Riccardo Redi, and Franco Venturini. 1953.

Hendricks, Gordon. **Origins of the American Film.** 1961-1966. New Introduction by Gordon Hendricks.

Hound and Horn: Essays on Cinema, 1928-1934. 1971.

Huff, Theodore. **Charlie Chaplin.** 1951.

Kahn, Gordon. **Hollywood on Trial.** 1948.

New York Times Film Reviews, 1913-1968. 1970.

Noble, Peter. **Hollywood Scapegoat: The Biography of Erich von Stroheim.** 1950.

Robson, E. W. and M. M. **The Film Answers Back.** 1939.

Seldes, Gilbert. **An Hour with the Movies and the Talkies.** 1929.

Weinberg, Herman G., editor. **Greed.** 1971.

Wollenberg, H. H. **Anatomy of the Film.** 1947.

Wright, Basil. **The Use of the Film.** 1948.

DISSERTATIONS ON FILM

Beaver, Frank Eugene. **Bosley Crowther: Social Critic of the Film, 1940-1967.** First publication, 1974.

Benderson, Albert Edward. **Critical Approaches to Federico Fellini's "8½".** First publication, 1974.

Cohen, Louis Harris. **The Cultural-Political Traditions and Developments of the Soviet Cinema: 1917-1972.** First publication, 1974.

Dart, Peter. **Pudovkin's Films and Film Theory.** First publication, 1974.

Facey, Paul W. **The Legion of Decency: A Sociological Analysis of the Emergence and Development of a Social Pressure Group.** First publication, 1974.

Karpf, Stephen L. **The Gangster Film: Emergence, Variation and Decay of a Genre, 1930-1940.** First publication, 1973.

Lounsbury, Myron O. **The Origins of American Film Criticism, 1909-1939.** First publication, 1973.

Lyons, Timothy James. **The Silent Partner: The History of the American Film Manufacturing Company, 1910-1921.** First publication, 1974.

McLaughlin, Robert. **Broadway and Hollywood: A History of Economic Interaction.** First publication, 1974.

North, Joseph H. **The Early Development of the Motion Picture, 1887-1909.** First publication, 1973.

Rimberg, John. **The Motion Picture in the Soviet Union, 1918-1952.** First publication, 1973.

Sands, Pierre N. **A Historical Study of the Academy of the Motion Picture Arts and Sciences (1927-1947).** First publication, 1973.

Wolfe, Glenn J. **Vachel Lindsay: The Poet as Film Theorist.** First publication, 1973.